A Par   Surviving the Teen Years

By Lee Brooks

The author acknowledges that only life experience has given her the ability to advise anyone about how to survive life with a teenager.

The author has no educational degrees to back up her skill, and encourages all who are seeking help to find a therapist they can love and trust just as she did.

Every effort has been made to maintain some semblance of privacy for the author's family. Names and even genders have been randomly assigned and all situations profiled are fictional.

Special thanks to Marcia Berman, Leslie Tsukroff, and Pamela Frueh for the sharing of their professional expertise with this book.

All scripture references are from the New Living Translation (NLT) unless otherwise noted.

Bibliographic credit appears at the end of this work.

To Marcia Berman

Who taught me how to use the tools I had more effectively and who helped me add so many more!

~ And ~

To The Women of Oasis 2013

Who asked such good questions that I just had to answer with this book.

I am a prisoner of hope.
Zechariah 9:12

Author Lee Brooks' Website:

www.authorleebrooks.webs.com

Author Lee Brooks' email:

authorleebrooks@gmail.com

Author Lee Brooks on Facebook:

www.facebook.com/authorleebrooks

Author Lee Brooks on Twitter:

www.twitter.com/authorleebrooks

Table of Contents

First Things First

I am not a psychologist, psychiatrist, or therapist nor do I have any training in these areas.

My qualification for writing this book is merely that I am the mother of teens who reached a point where extensive professional help through hospitalization, therapy, and medication had to be sought.

I write this book because the things I learned through this difficult experience _worked_ and my life is now _significantly better_ as a result. This is my only qualification and I strongly, _strongly_ encourage anyone who is struggling with difficult situations at home between you and your teen to seek professional help immediately. I can claim success only as a result of years spent with qualified therapists. (Note: I'm talking about more than one!)

The next section provides a brief insight into our family's struggles.

But the more the Egyptians oppressed them, the more the Israelites multiplied and spread, and the more alarmed the Egyptians became. ... Then Pharaoh gave this order to all his people: "Throw every newborn Hebrew boy into the Nile River. But you may let the girls live."

About this time, a man and woman from the tribe of Levi got married. The woman became pregnant and gave birth to a son. She saw that he was a special baby and kept him hidden for three months. But when she could no longer hide him, she got a basket made of papyrus reeds and waterproofed it with tar and pitch. She put the baby in the basket and laid it among the reeds along the bank of the Nile River. The baby's sister then stood at a distance, watching to see what would happen to him.

Exodus 1:12, 22, 2:1-4

I can understand some of the emotions that Jochebed went through. I wonder how many times she wanted to fist her hands, stomp her feet, and scream at the top of her lungs, "I DON'T WANT TO DO THIS ANYMORE!"

Like Jochebed, I knew all about the inescapable evil of the world trying to destroy all that I held precious and dear. Like Jochebed, I experienced the kind of fear that kept me awake at night, rooted in the fear of failure to save a child. Like Jochebed, I battled the frustration that ate at me from the inside out over my utter inability to do anything to fix the nightmare I was living. And like Jochebed, I suffered the misery of realizing that I had reached the end of my rope and knew the only thing I could possibly do was surrender.

I also understand how Jochebed continued to get out of bed each morning and put one foot in front of the other. It came after I reached a point of such utter despair that I knew that only God's guidance could offer me a solution ... as unpalatable as it seemed. The point of surrender for me was not relief, but an agonizing collapse in the realization that by earthly standards I had lost, I had failed, and there was absolutely nothing else I could possibly do to save what I held so very precious. The first bright light in the midst of the nightmare was remembering the core focus of who I was as a woman: God's Own.

Jochebed decided to fashion a basket and float her baby down a crocodile infested river trusting that God would keep him safe. I decided to put my child in a locked-down psychiatric hospital trusting that God would keep that child safe.

Just like Jochebed, I determined to be thankful in the midst of things: for prayer warrior friends and family, for good doctors and understanding nurses, for health insurance, for a strong marriage, for God's tacit presence even at three in the morning in the hospital emergency facility ... And just like Jochebed, I determined to stand on God's promises for my life and for my child's.

The blessing that Jochebed's baby boy became to humanity took many lifetimes to be fully appreciated. In fact, we're still basking in the blessing that was Moses' life and his legacy. Just like Jochebed I have decided not to expect to see my child's full blessings in my lifetime; why aim small?

Endless prayer, helpful medication, intense individual therapy, painful joint therapy, hours of personal research, and the addition of new and improved coping techniques to my personal coping toolbox became essential components to surviving daily life. Already I see an incredible improvement: a child who is healthier and stronger, I who am healthier and stronger, and a family that is healthier and stronger. Who would have thought that such a family crisis could result in such a positive outcome? God's love and blessings continue to shine, making those dark days and months and years something that I now understand were vital and necessary to get to the better place we are at today.

Would I want to repeat those dark days?
Absolutely not! But I can already be thankful that
today we are: better, stronger, wiser, and better
prepared. I look at my child and feel … hope again.
I look at myself and feel … optimism again. Yes, I'm
battered and I'm bruised. My sword is a little
bloody around the edges. But I'm upright and I'm
smiling at the fierce feeling of … ability. God is with
me! God loves me! God will not abandon me!
God will make all things work towards good!

Look at me, everyone, rising out of the fire. My life
has taught me to be excited about the future!

I'm God's Own. With Him I can do anything.

Things I Did That Were Wrong

1. I thought I was the only one with serious problems in my family. I thought that while everyone complained about being the parents of teens, no one had gotten it as wrong as I had or had as serious a problem as I did.

2. I blamed myself for the state of our family and the problems we faced, and wasted a lot of time second guessing myself. I thought, "I should have done this instead of that ..." By second guessing myself and my parenting techniques I lost self-confidence. As I lost self-confidence I became depressed over my ignorance and failures.

3. We didn't get professional help quickly enough for our teens. Initial significant warning signs were ignored in the hopes that they would simply go away or heal themselves. What warning signs you ask? How about a death threat to a teacher? Despite the advice of a trusted school counselor to seek professional counseling for our teen, we waited another two years.

4. I didn't get professional help quickly enough for myself. Even after the hospitalization of my teen, I still held back despite numerous well-meaning friends and family who

encouraged me to "find someone to talk to." I only went as a last, desperate resort. In my first session, after I told my whole, sorry story, Marcia said to me, "Well, I've been in the business for almost thirty years and I think you might be the first family I've ever encountered that got it right with their teen the first time around." Her words made me feel a thousand pounds lighter and was the beginning of regaining my self-confidence back as a parent.

5.   I doubted the power of prayer on more than one occasion, believing that my teen was lost to us and that things would never improve. I doubted that our family would ever be healed. My prayer team (one good thing that I did) never doubted, however, and "shored me up" numerous times when I desperately needed it.

6.   For a period of time I forgot Who was in charge and believed the difficult diagnosis we received that painted a bleak, hopeless future for my child. While my prayer partners championed God's power and maintained their optimism, in the deepest part of my heart there were times when I had little hope.

Things I Did That Were Right

1. I viewed therapy as something I needed to educate me further and help me be a more successful human being. I treated it like going to college: I learned about myself and my weakness, about my marriage and its weaknesses, and my parenting style and its weaknesses. I gained powerful insight on how to make all of it better. (Picture me with a determined glint in my eye saying, "Look out world.")

2. I asked a million questions and kept asking them until I understood everything I needed to understand. Initially, most information I was given sounded like a foreign language. I was polite, sincere, and determined to understand as much as I could.

3. I researched the medications that our teens were given on the Internet and made phone calls to trusted people in the medical and counseling field. I picked their brains and asked for their advice.

4. I took detailed notes and kept diligent records. I recorded dates, names, locations, and quotes that people said to me. I printed out important stuff that I needed to save and filed it in an accordion folder. Whenever appropriate, I asked for

photocopies. I went into all meetings with My Notebook.

5. I shared from every session with Marcia and my husband my new and improved tools for dealing with our teen. When we ran into complications at home, I took it as a victory when my husband would say to me, "Uh oh. You better discuss this with Marcia the next time you see her."

6. I had a trusted group of close family and friends who knew the whole story and whom I could call and talk to and ask for prayer at any time.

7. I made full disclosure to all people who had a supervisory position over my teens. I wanted them to know that my teens needed special care because I wanted them to be on my side to help my teens succeed. I said on more than one occasion, "Put a big red flag on my teen's folder. I want everyone who deals with my teen to know the full situation and call me if they have any questions."

8. I met with my teens' therapists and school counselors on my own every few months to make sure they had an accurate perception (or at least *my* perception) of what I believed was true reality.

9. I held fast with God, although at times I believed the bleak diagnosis we were given and the grim prognosis for the future. I continued to pray and to ask for prayer

even though I held little hope of a positive outcome.

10. I was determined to do my best to have no regrets regarding my decisions. I took the diagnosis I was given for my teens and worked positively toward the best case scenario I could achieve. I recognized that I was a smart, intelligent, determined woman and that I must continue to act in an exemplary, wise fashion. (I didn't want there to <u>ever</u> be a point in the future where I thought, "Oh, I wish I had done that...").

11. I counted on God to help us through it all. (Picture me with my hands on my hips, tapping my foot impatiently and asking, "What do I need to do to get through this God?")

On Therapy and Therapists

Therapy is popular with no one (Marcia says, except if you live in Manhattan!). There's the inconvenience of having to find someone you trust, trying to find time in your already extremely busy schedule, the added hardship of payment should insurance not cover the treatment, and the general stigma attributed to the phrase, "I'm seeing a therapist."

I sought therapy because I reached a point in my life where I felt I had no option: I was Desperate with a capital "D". I believed that I was a complete and utter failure as a mother and was incapable of fixing the nightmare that was playing regularly in my home. Despite my success as a teacher, despite my solid marriage, despite my strong faith, despite my supportive family, despite my relatively stable life, despite my positive emotional outlook ... yes despite all those things, my home was being torn apart at the seams. Desperation, panic, and real honest-to-goodness fear had invaded the four walls of my home and I knew of no way to fix things.

Brief hospitalization for my teen and years (yes, years) of therapy for a significant portion of my family have brought me to the good place that I am at today. I feel in control, confident, and optimistic about my family's future. I am joyful in the relationships I have reestablished with my children.

I am capable of handling just about any situation that happens in my home now in a successful, healthy manner.

I shared much of my story in my *God's Phoenix Woman* Conference and had many women come up to me afterwards and ask, "Which book addresses the problems you had with your teens?" It was that question that prompted me to write this book.

But please – I beg you – find a therapist you trust and begin your own journey to health and happiness! I cannot adequately communicate how vitally important it is to have someone you trust answer questions like: Why didn't this work? Why did this work? What should I have done better? What would have been a better way to approach this problem? Why did I get so annoyed over such a trivial thing? If your sincerity, will, and dedication to your family has not enabled you to succeed thus far, reading my little book isn't going to help much either. You need the skills and perceptions of specialists *from outside your home* to help you rebuild what is broken. If you get nothing else out of this book, let it at least be the wise decision to seek outside help.

Now if you know someone who is seeing a therapist they like, start there. Word of mouth is more reliable than the way I found mine, (as successful as that turned out).

Surprisingly, I found my therapist on the Internet. Don't laugh. I was at the stage where I didn't want to start asking everyone, "Hey, do you know a good therapist?" but I was desperate enough that I knew I had to do something. I googled therapists and up popped "Psychology Today: Find a Therapist, Psychologist, Counselor" and I clicked on the link. I searched by my home city (who wants to drive far, right?), and started scrolling through the choices. There were actual photographs of most of the therapists listed, professional titles (SEE Therapy Resources), and personal paragraphs that had been written by each of the therapists profiled. I prayed that God would help me find a good one and then I chose three I liked and made the phone calls. All my calls went immediately to voicemail so I bit the bullet and left my name and phone number. I prayed again that God would give me clear direction regarding the best choice.

The first one who called only wanted to talk about what insurance I carried. She never asked me why I was seeking a therapist, and quite frankly, while I know money is important it left a bad taste in my mouth. She didn't have an appointment opening for four weeks and I decided to call her back only as a last resort. The second therapist was polite but had no availability for new patients and encouraged me to call back in six to eight weeks. By the third therapist I was getting a little bit discouraged (already!). She asked me why I wanted to see a therapist and I told her briefly what was going on in my life. "Oh honey," she said, "let's get you in here ASAP! How does Tuesday look for you?" I'd found my therapist, Marcia!

I found out later how good God was to me to send Marcia so quickly. Finding therapists for my teens was a struggle, and we had numerous fits and starts until we finally found one that worked.

Please note that my teens were *never* as enthusiastic about seeing a therapist as I was. As we went through the selection process, I allowed input regarding whether my teens felt a connection or not with the therapists in question, but the only option was always to find another if that one was not a good fit. (The option to *not* seeing a therapist was not given.) I do believe that half the battle about my teens seeing therapists was already won, however, because I, too, was seeing one. The stigma of "I'm seeing a therapist because I'm broken/crazy/the problem" was mitigated by my enthusiastically attending my own sessions as well. (I didn't realize it but I'd already started using a tool! SEE Looking In The Mirror)

The key to finding a good therapist is twofold: 1.) Do not give up, *and* 2.) Do not settle. Give any therapist two sessions. If you are getting nothing out of the time and money you are investing, move on. With Marcia, I benefitted immediately.

When I searched for a therapist, I wasn't even aware that there were different kinds based on their schooling, qualifications and styles of therapy. At the end of this booklet is a section entitled "Therapy Resources" if you'd like to know more about that. The variations in qualifications and different methods of therapy can be

On Therapy And Therapists   [14]

overwhelming, which is the last thing you need at
this time, so only go there if you need clarification.

> *In times of trouble, may the LORD
> answer your cry.*
>
> *May the name of ... God ... keep
> you safe from all harm.*
>
> *May He send you help from His
> sanctuary and strengthen you ...*
>
> *Psalm 20:1-3*

Embracing the Truth of Teens:

1. A large majority of parents cannot effectively meet the emotional needs of their teenagers. Blame can be placed only on parents who make no effort to remedy this situation.

2. As far as teenagers are concerned, rarely are parents right in any argument, and nothing a parent can do will change that opinion.

3. The start of adolescence is not really defined by age (13) but by developmental maturity. The moment your teen begins to show the physical signs of maturity (and sometimes – GASP - even before the physical signs begin to show), you can have a teenager on your hands. This can be as early as 10. (Sorry, but someone had to tell you.)

4. They told you that parenthood was hard. They were right. They told you that raising a teen was the hardest. They were right. This is your final exam. Unfortunately it's pass/fail.

5. Although your teen may be bigger than you and smarter than you in certain areas, he or she is still in an important stage of learning,

and you are still in the vital stage of teaching.

6. Teenagers are like supertankers, not speedboats – they take a really long, slow time to turn around. Forget about immediate results.

7. You, your teen, and your family will never achieve perfection nor should you even attempt that goal. Striving to <u>Get It Right</u> is the highest ideal to aim for.

8. You are part of the problem. That's the bad news. The good news is that you're wiser, smarter, more experienced, and more powerful. When you fix your end by improving your skills, modifying your behaviors, and better understanding this wild creature in your house, half the battle is already won.

9. Building up your teens' self-esteem is the best thing you can do for everyone. Your teens need to learn to value themselves as individuals. Comparison is rarely healthy. Remember, a son relates more closely with his father and a daughter relates more closely with her mother.

10. Believe that God is in control of every situation that is occurring with you and your teens. He is greater than anything this world can provide.

*May God give you more and more
mercy, peace, and love.*

Jude 1:2

Families

All families are individually unique and each possesses its own strengths and weaknesses. Throughout this book you will get a vivid glimpse of my family as I detail the lengthy list of crises we worked to overcome. In all probability, your family is nothing like mine. (SEE My Family Then & Now if you want specific details.)

What you must remember is that regardless of my family situation we were in severe crisis. Complete failure was imminent. Regardless of what I did or did not have, at the worst moments we were not able to fix what was so desperately broken. I needed specialized help and God helped me find it. I asked and searched and called and persisted until I received the help my family required.

God will help you, too. He goes before you to prepare your path, walks beside you to befriend you and behind you to encourage you, is above you to watch over you and beneath you to carry you in troubled times and, most importantly, He is within you to give you His abiding love, mercy, and peace. Believe this. Know this. Rely on this.

I am not worthy of all the unfailing love and faithfulness you have shown to me, your servant.

Genesis 32:10

How To Get Out Of Bed Each Morning

When I was a young mother of three going through the sleeplessness of infancy and then the manic-ness of toddlerhood, it annoyed me to have parents of teens look at me, sigh, and say in a  voice filled with wistfulness, "Oh how I miss those days! You have no idea how lucky you are right now. Wait until they become teenagers." Now I feel compelled to submit a formal apology to all those parents about whom I grumbled under my breath.

There were many, many days when things fell apart with my teens and I just did not want to get out of bed. (One of my greatest escapes – next to getting lost in my Kindle or my computer – is sleep.) When I did manage to get out of bed, there was many a day where I wanted to fist my hands, stomp my feet, and scream up at God, "I DON'T WANT TO DO THIS!!!" (Somewhat childish but true.)

UNFORTUNATE FACT: Adolescence is the longest, most difficult stage your child will go through.

REALITY: Knowing that fact doesn't make us feel any better or make surviving it any easier.

TOOL: Count Your Blessings

Sitting in the hospital administration booth filling out forms that would commit one of my teens, for one instant through my real life nightmare I was overwhelmed with relief. The caseworker deliberately ignored my sobs and just kept passing me paper after paper after paper loaded with information that I did not have the mental or emotional capacity to comprehend. But one form stood out. "This form states that your present insurance carrier covers the entire seven day stay. You don't even have any co-pay." For the first time she looked me in the eye. "Lucky you," she finally said. "I guess I've got something to be thankful for," I finally managed through my tears. She responded, "Honey, you have *no idea.*"

I made a decision then and there that instead of listing all the things that were going wrong (and there were plenty of them), I'd start keeping a list in my head of all the things that were going right. It truly helped. Eventually, I started writing them down because the list got too lengthy and I was afraid I'd forget some. These blessings included: supportive husband, solid prayer warrior friends and family, doctors that I had confidence in, and even the fact that I got a bed in a preferred hospital without too long a wait ('only' 22 hours in the hospital emergency lock down wing). I later found out that some people can wait over 72 hours for a bed *anywhere*.

No matter how dark things are, don't forget to be thankful. The Lord goes before you, always.

> *"For I know the plans I have for you,:*
> *says the LORD. "They are plans for*
> *good and not for disaster, to give you a*
> *future and a hope."*
>
> *Jeremiah 29:11*

TOOL: Commit To Prayer

Let prayer take on a new meaning for you, even if you've never done it before, or simply never valued it for the powerful tool that it is. Commit to talk to God *all the time*, when you're terrified, confused, worried, angry, frustrated, or happy. Believe that He is waiting for you to contact Him to ask for His advice and assistance. Know that He has gone before you to prepare things and ease your way, and that He is beside you so that you are never alone. Ask Him questions. Tell Him your worries. List your needs.

Remember to keep your prayer time balanced. Don't spend the whole time asking for things. It helps to list the things you are thankful for that God has already put in place for you. Prayer is:

    1. Thanksgivings and

2. Requests.

Remember to pray for:

1. <u>You and your partner</u>: for God's clear direction and guidance, for unity, for wisdom, for patience.

2. <u>Your teens</u>: for God's clear direction and guidance, for wisdom, for patience, for a heart open and willing to listen to God

3. <u>Your teens' caregivers</u> (teachers, therapist, etc.) and friends.

4. <u>Your support team</u>: here's a place to be thankful! (SEE Build A Support Team)

Prayer is a vital tool that you must make full use of. Perhaps during this time in your life you will finally be convinced of its tremendous value and power.

> *Do not be afraid or discouraged, for the Lord will personally go ahead of you.*
>
> *Deuteronomy 31:8a*

<u>**TOOL: Build A Support Team**</u>

You cannot do this alone. You and your partner cannot do this alone. Your family cannot do this alone. You must ask for help. If you are not good at doing that and feel guilty receiving help, commit to yourself that once all this is over you will do something in return to communicate your gratitude to these valuable people God has put in your life. Here is a core group I suggest:

1. <u>Prayer Warriors</u>: Find people who will pray for you and your family. You need to keep them updated as things change.

2. <u>Shoulders To Cry On</u>: Find people who will be willing to listen to you and support you. This list needs to include YOUR THERAPIST. In addition, it might include people that you trust and love. (They may be part of your prayer warrior team.)

3. <u>Emergency Assistance</u>: Find people who will be there in a pinch to help pick someone up from soccer practice, be there when the washing machine is delivered, make you a mean cup of tea when you simply have to get out of the house, leave work early to go with you to the hospital to commit your teen, and leave an occasional freshly baked crumb cake on your front porch.

These groups don't have to be separate; but they have to *be.* Recognize them for what they are: part of God's blessing to you in your life and evidence that He has gone before you to prepare things for you for this exact situation. It did not escape my notice that God had gone before me and provided me with a friend in the medical field, a friend who had already struggled with serious issues with a teen, a friend who was Internet savvy,

a sister who was strong and opinionated, a minister
who was both a friend and spiritual advisor, a
mother and father who were champion prayer
warriors, and a husband who had the ability to
provide care and support no matter where he was
traveling in the world. Don't hesitate to ask those
God has given you for help and support. Someday
you will probably be just as important for them.

*Enjoy the companionship of those who
call on the Lord with pure hearts.*

2 Timothy 2:21-23

TOOL: Refuse To Give Up

With God on your side you are bigger, stronger,
and wiser than anything this world can throw at
you. Anything. You may not believe this in the
crisis of the moment, but this is true. By having a
spiritual center, a belief that God is with you and
will not leave you no matter what, you can build a
foundation that cannot be destroyed, and have an
outlook that is filled with hope. Think of people
you know who inspired you in the way they faced
hardships. Do you think they always viewed
themselves as heroes or motivational speakers or
brave warriors? Of course they didn't. They were
simply struggling human beings *just like you* who
refused to give up no matter how bleak the future
appeared to be.

Write the following verse down and put it in your wallet. When you write it down, make sure to underline the word "everything" and take a moment to realize what that word entails. This is a promise from God.

And we know that God causes
everything to work together for the good
of those who love God and are called
according to His purpose for them.

Romans 8:28

TOOL: Embrace Reality

Don't live in denial. Denial makes you stupid. Denial leads you to make wrong decisions. Denial postpones doing the right thing and causes problems to get bigger and worse. Be hopefully realistic.

1. Be prayerful. It helps keep your perspective aimed in the right direction.

2. Be patient. Nothing ever happens as fast as we want it to. God's time is different than our time. Don't let anyone force you into snap decisions.

3. Be observant. Watch for evidence of God's direction. Watch for evidence of God's care for you. Listen for God's still small voice. I always pray for "big, black arrows." I'm rather ignorant and clueless as I walk around trying to find God's direction for me

and my life. If I could only figure out where He wants me to go, I'd be glad to do it. So I ask God to paint big, black arrows continually and I'll happily follow them.

4. <u>Be committed to wise decisions</u>. You are out to do what you believe is best for you and your family. If too many people are giving you differing opinions, go away by yourself, be quiet, and pray. Go through each of your options and ask the Lord to make you feel a guided certainty about the direction you should take.

"Yes, my teen is in the hospital for emotional reasons. Yes, I'm feeling rather ill prepared to face this nightmare. But I am not alone. I have God, friends, and family supporting me. With God's guidance, I will make the decision that I believe to be the wisest."

Show me your intentions so I will understand You more fully and do exactly what You want me to do.
Exodus 33:13

TOOL: Putting The Baby In The Basket

Jochebed was Moses' mother. Most of us know the Bible story about how she floated her baby down the river in a woven basket and how Pharaoh's daughter found the baby and everyone lived happily ever after.

But take a moment to think about the story from Jochebed's point of view. She was so desperate that she put her three month old baby in a crocodile infested river and left her young daughter to watch over him. That must have been a time of some astronomical desperation, don't you think? We don't even let our children sit in our kitchens in their highchairs these days without firmly strapping them in.

I've come to view Jochebed's decision of putting her baby in that basket as her absolutely giving up control and giving it all to God. I did exactly the same thing when I signed the committal papers that put my teen in a psychiatric hospital. Sometimes life brings us to the point of being completely helpless. That's when we take that leap of faith into God's loving arms.

Listen to me clearly; doing that is *not* giving up, it is giving our problem to God. Sometimes life brings us to that point. That's all we can do and it's exactly what God needs us to do. You are never alone.

How To Get Out Of Bed In The Morning   [28]

So here's what I want you to do, God helping you:

Take your everyday, ordinary life — your sleeping, eating, going-to-work, and walking-around life — and place it before God as an offering.

Let God change the way you think.

Embracing what God does for you is the best thing you can do for Him.

Then you will learn to know God's will for you, which is good and pleasing and perfect.

Romans 12:2 (NLT & MSG)

How To Change Your Perspective

You desperately want your teens to understand where you are coming from: you love them and you want the best for them. You have a lifetime of experience to share with them: you want to make their lives  easier, you want them to learn from your mistakes! You are determined to do what's best for them whether they like it or not.

That's *your* perspective and according to your teens you're welcome to it.

Can you articulate your teens' perspective as sincerely? If you cannot understand where they are coming from don't expect them to understand you.

They think they are right and they believe you are wrong; that's *their* perspective.

UNFORTUNATE FACT: Teenagers think differently than anyone else on the planet. There is very little a parent can do to counteract this aside from waiting for them to change into something other than teenagers. That could take years.

REALITY: You must try to understand them in order to be able to coexist happily with them until this much anticipated change finally happens.

TOOL: Forgiveness

I was angry for a long time. I suppose if you wanted a list of reasons, you would have seen that I was somewhat justified. There was a piece of me that held on with white knuckles and gritted teeth to the future time when I would be vindicated. I wanted to hear any one or all of the following: "You were right," or "I'm so very sorry, Mom," or "Thanks you saved me," or "I wouldn't be here without you," or "I know I screwed up, thanks for not giving up on me."

In order for me, my teen, and my family to move forward in a direction that was happy, healthy, and whole I needed to let that attitude go. Giving it up to God meant that He was in charge of it all. I couldn't add stipulations. I needed to get off my high horse of superiority (which my teen regularly complained about.)

> "You always think you're right! You're not!"

I had to embrace the truth that God was with us and was in control. I had to admit that the forgiveness I counted on from Him for my many failures was just as significant. I had to stop being so self-righteous. My teen was His gift to me and I wasn't called to be proven right, I was called to *get it right*. If you expect forgiveness from your teen, you've got to practice it yourself. Forgive.

> *Make allowance for each other's faults,*
> *and forgive anyone who offends you.*
> *Remember, the Lord forgave you, so*
> *you must forgive others. Above all,*
> *clothe yourselves with love, which binds*
> *us all together in perfect harmony.*
> *And let the peace that comes from*
> *Christ rule in your hearts. For as*
> *members of one body you are called to*
> *live in peace. And always be*
> *thankful.*
>
> *Colossians 3:13-15*

<u>TOOL: Understanding Fear!</u>

> *I prayed to the Lord, and He*
> *answered me. He freed me from all*
> *my fears.*
>
> *Psalm 34:4*

Teenagers, though they are often unable to recognize it or verbalize it, are motivated almost exclusively by fear: fear of failure, fear of the unknown, etc. Embracing this truth and operating based on this truth is essential for parental success. (And please don't bother asking your teens if they are afraid, they'll deny it.)

The second important fact within this concept is that teenagers rarely react towards fear as adults expect. Fear of failure is often dealt with by simply not trying at all.

> "Why bother trying? I'm not going to get it right anyway."

Fear of being alone is often handled by becoming as difficult and contrary as possible.

> "Why should I care what you think or how you feel? I know you hate me already."

Become your teens' champion and advocate. Search out ways for them to be successful. Use positive words whenever possible, and work to help them feel secure. They need someone on their side; be that person.

Good parents must learn to be contrary, too, but in a positive way! Hate the behavior, not the teen. Be frustrated with the situation, not the teen. Be angry with the unavoidable circumstances, not the teen. Understand that fear fuels anger. Ask "How can I allay these fears?" If it helps, remember how you felt when your teens were cute, lovable and little, crying in the middle of the night out of fear. It is unfortunate that in some ways little children can be more articulate regarding what they need than teens.

<u>TOOL: Living In The Moment</u>

My child, listen to me and do as I say, and you will have a long, good life. I will teach you wisdom's ways and lead you in straight paths. When you walk, you won't be held back; when you run, you won't stumble.

Proverbs 4:10-12

Teenagers operate almost exclusively in the moment. Even though their futures are in front of them, they rarely seem capable of comprehending it or planning for it. (That ability comes with maturity.) Parental attempts to speed this process along through lengthy discussions are usually met with derision ("You'll never understand!") dismissal ("It's not like it was when you were a kid!") and anger ("I hate you and your advice!"). Oh yes, and let's not forget the exaggerated eye roll.

<u>Stop fighting the tide and determine to operate based upon your own experience and common sense.</u> Your teens will not see your side of things. Realize that teens live in the moment and that's the way they view the world during this phase of their lives. (SEE My Reality vs. My Teen's Reality.)

> "I don't feel comfortable with your sleeping over Katie's. I've never met her and you've only just recently started speaking about her. Let's have the first sleepover here. Get her mom's phone number and I'll give her a call and set it up. I'm even happy to pick Katie up if that's easier for her family. Let me know."

Don't doubt yourself. You've made your mistakes and (hopefully!) you've learned from them. You know what your teens are capable of and not capable of. You know what the world offers: the good, the bad, and the ugly. Embrace your reality and don't let denial make you stupid. (SEE Embrace Reality.) Let your decisions be based on prayer and wisdom.

> "I appreciate that you want me to drop you off at the mall unsupervised for the afternoon. I'm not comfortable with that. If you'd like, I'm willing to go along and sit and read my book for *two hours* this afternoon. Think about it and let me know."

Model behavior you'd like them to exhibit. It will give them a good example to follow and will give you a solid foundation to build on.

> "I understand that you want a boa constrictor. You're welcome to get one once you're living on your own and can assume all the responsibilities that go along with owning a pet like that."

Notice that many of the above examples end in *'Let me know.'* You are not always issuing an order; sometimes you are offering an option. It gives your teens some power in how the situation will play out, but on your terms. Perhaps they may come back with a variation of your suggestion that you might be willing to realistically consider. (SEE Compromise and Cooperation.)

TOOL: Try To Remember

How were your teen years? Smooth as silk? Perhaps they were a wonderful example of love and communication between parent and teen? Is it something you'd be willing to relive again? Chances are your adolescence was not perfect. Even if your situation was vastly different from your teen's, I'd encourage you to make an effort to remember the feelings, emotions, and struggles you dealt with. A little empathy can go a long way.

I must express my anguish. My bitter soul must complain.

Job 7:11

TOOL: Being Wrong

"You think you know everything! You think you're never wrong!"

I'm sorry to break it to you, but you're not perfect and, in addition, you're not right all the time. Acknowledging that to yourself and (gasp!) to your teens might cause a huge shift in your relationship.

"I know I don't always do the right thing. I know I make mistakes. I am trying to be the best Mom possible to you. I will listen more closely to what you say to me. Please do the same with me."

TOOL: Asking Advice

"You are so much better at electronics than I am. Can you help me figure out how to order a new battery for my phone?"

If you want to see your teens blossom, put them in a position where you acknowledge that they are capable. Choose any area that you're comfortable in, whether it is a job around the house, a talent

they shine in, or personal skill they have that
impresses you, and talk it up.

> "Do you remember how you fixed that special
> spaghetti sauce? It was delicious. I'd love to
> have you do it again."

Or:

> "I can't do this right. Can you try?"

TOOL: Land Your Helicopter

Think about your greatest learning experiences.
Think about the times when you drew closer to
God. Think about the times you really appreciated
adult assistance. All of those times were probably
difficult and stressful. Triumph can only come
about as a result of struggle. Victory can only come
about from battle. Feeling successful can only
come about from *having tried.* Let 'em get a little
bit battered and dirty. They'll appreciate it more
when they *call out to you* and you come and ...
maybe not rescue them but help them stand and
brush themselves off.

WRONG: "Jim, remember to put your homework
in your back pack and don't forget your clean gym

clothes. Did you find the new deodorant I left on your dresser? Oh, and I called your science teacher about the low grade you got on the homework that I checked. She was completely out of line and I told her so..."

RIGHT:

"Well, before I jump in with my many suggestions as usual, what do <u>you</u> think would be the best solution?"

Or:

"Tell me how I can help you. What do you need from me?"

And listen. If your teens decline your assistance, respect their decision. "Let me know if you change your mind" is always a good final response.

TOOL: Praise

Praise goes a long way. Praise builds, encourages, and strengthens. In addition, it's important to have conversations with your teens that are not laced with tension or hidden agendas. Commit to finding at least one thing a day that you can say to your teens that is positive. That might take a bit of effort and change of perspective, but it can be done. It can be as simple as complementing their perfume, praising the fact that they remembered to bring in the garbage cans without having to be asked, or liking a song you heard them playing.

"How do you get your eyeliner to look so smooth? It always looks so professional."

Or:

"You're good at foreign languages in school."

Or:

"Your lit essay was fabulous! What a great topic. Good job!"

Let someone else praise you, not your own mouth.

Proverbs 27:2

There isn't an effective plan in place that doesn't have solid rules or guidelines. Your family should be like that. On the other hand, there is not an effective plan in place that doesn't allow for flexibility, utilize  the unique strengths of each individual involved, and continually evaluates itself for areas of improvement. Your family should be like that, too.

UNFORTUNATE FACT: Teenagers can often cause unimaginable worry, stress, and tension in a family.

REALITY: You can't escape this worry, stress, and tension because *it lives with you,* and you are legally responsible for caring for your teens until they are at least 18 years of age.

TOOL: The Unbreakable Box

Come up with your own set of standards (different from every day rules that allows the possibility of changing) that nothing – *and I mean nothing* will cause you to compromise. This set of standards should be brief, easy to articulate, easy to remember and recite without having to think. In addition, these standards should be supported by the other adults in authority in your home, and should apply to *all other youth of similar age range and status.* No double standards.

Once you have this list, never deviate from it. Let it be your manifesto; the place you look to when all other things are being considered. Although you may, over the course of time, refine it, the essence of these standards should never change.

I was encouraged to come up with my unbreakable box of rules because I regularly felt powerless, confused, and unhappy in my home. On a daily basis I was faced with situations over which I felt that I had no control. And I had no idea how to fix any of them. That's when Marcia explained about boundaries. But I liked the mental image of a box that surrounded me. Inside the box were all the things I needed to have to be calm, peaceful, and in control. Outside of the box was ... well outside of the box, and I acknowledged that I had no control there.

Here are examples of my standards:

1. <u>My teenager's reality will never trump my reality.</u>

> "I appreciate that's your reality. However, my reality is different and I don't feel comfortable with this plan."

Or:

> "I appreciate your argument. However, we agreed that you would not be allowed to get your learner's permit until your grades had improved enough to qualify for a good driver's insurance discount."

2. <u>I will never make snap decisions about important things.</u> I will always take time to pray, think, and discuss with those I trust before I make a key decision.

> "I'll need to think and pray about this. I'll need to discuss this with Dad. I'll get back to you."

Or:

> "If you need an immediate answer it will have to be no. I haven't had a chance to think and pray about this. I haven't had a chance to talk with Dad about this. I won't be rushed into making important decisions."

3. <u>Safety is always my primary concern.</u>

> "I'm not comfortable with this, and keeping you safe is my primary concern. The answer is no."

Or:

> "No. I don't feel comfortable with your
> going over to Madeline's house. Last time,
> her mother didn't respect our rules about
> curfew."

Or:

> "Good for you. You've thought ahead about
> all the things that you know I worry about and
> have come up with a good solution to each
> one. I knew I could count on you! Sure, you
> can go."

4. I will follow the laws of society.

> "No. Underage drinking is against the law."

Or:

> "No. I will not lie to Andrea's parents about
> where you are going tonight. If you'd like, I'll
> speak with them and tell them why I was
> willing to let you go."

Or:

> "No, you cannot drive with Mary Lou. She already has her sister in the car and the law states she can only have one other teen in the car with her when she is driving. I'll be happy to take you and pick you up."

TOOL: Getting To The Punchline

Many of the examples in the previous tool, The Unbreakable Box, deal with a specific issue, yet do not address the all-important punchline: the conclusion that needs to be drawn to offer an opportunity for success *the next time*.

> "If you need an immediate answer it will have to be no. I haven't had a chance to think and pray about this. I haven't had a chance to talk with Dad about this. I won't be rushed in making important decisions. "

What's the punchline to this situation? The punchline is that your teen should give you more time to think about important decisions. As a parent, you might be inclined to say, "And furthermore, next time a situation like this arises, I'd advise you to speak with me well in advance. You know how Dad and I..."

It is far more effective to guide your teens to that punchline and have them voice it themselves:

TEEN: Great. I never get to do anything.

YOU: Please think ahead about what you need to do in the future so we can avoid this happening again.

Here's another example:

> "No, that's too expensive. We can't afford to buy that.

You might be inclined to add the punchline: "You need to be better with saving your money" or, "Remember how Lesley saved money for her bicycle? We could do that."

TEEN: I never get anything. All the other kids have one.

YOU: Well, if this is so important, think about what you could do to get one. You know I'm always willing to negotiate.

Helping your teens learn to come up with their own solutions to problems is a valuable skill they will use throughout their lifetime.

TOOL: Consistency

Always be consistent, even if your teens think it's consistently annoying. Don't let tears, whining, or cajoling weaken your resolve. Believe in your reality (SEE My Reality vs. My Teen's), rely on your unbreakable box of standards (SEE The Unbreakable Box). In addition, make sure your partner is consistent as well. (SEE The United Front.)

> *The Lord is my strength and shield. I trust Him with all my heart. He helps me, and my heart is filled with joy.*
> *Psalm 28:7*

TOOL: Forward Thinking

We have three children, and for a period we had three teens in our house! My husband and I *never* made a rule for one teen without thinking ahead into the future for the others. We kept this forward thinking attitude regarding rewards and privileges also.

> "That's not fair. You didn't do that for Lesley when she used to be late from her dates."

Don't for one second think that any of the drama that is occurring under your roof is escaping other family members' attention. The younger ones watch carefully and remember everything. They observe how you present the rules, how well you uphold the rules, and how firmly you adhere to the consequences. How you behave with one teen can make it easier – or harder – for your other teens as they come along. Be determined to get it right.

Whenever a major incident occurred we sat down as a family and explained the facts and what the consequences were going to be. We tried to be open and honest with all who were affected within the household.

> "I'm sure you can tell that I've been very upset since I received that phone call this afternoon. Franchesca's counselor from school called today and she's been suspended from school for threatening another student on the bus. Franchesca must go to in-school suspension for the rest of this week. We will be going in to talk more with school officials in the morning. As for here at home, she will also be grounded for the same amount of time she is suspended – including loss of phone and Internet privileges. Additionally, she won't be able to go to the concert that she's been looking forward to. No one is happy right now."

TOOL: Not The Same, Always Fair

Shockingly, one of the biggest mistakes my husband and I made was treating all three of our teens the same way. We did everything in our power to not favor one teen over another and to have the same rules for all. When everything fell apart, we struggled with the reality: How come our rules worked so well with two of our children but not the third?

We learned that, despite our best intentions, we were actually making it worse by failing to modify certain rules. Ironically, with just a little bit of tweaking on the delivery, we didn't have to compromise our principals at all.

Let me give you an example. The rule in our home was that in order to get a cell phone, you had to prove to be conscientious with your school/homework first. No problem for two out of three of our teens. But it became a huge problem when a younger teen earned a phone that an older one still hadn't.

Ironically, our rule began to work against us. Our phoneless teen would go out with friends and … we couldn't get in touch. Worse yet, our teen had saved money and bought an IPOD with WIFI capabilities and was able to communicate with friends freely – reaching a point where a phone wasn't necessary. The irony was that I wanted that teen to have a phone so that I could communicate more easily. (Our school district allows phone communication between classes, and it was a convenience I wanted with all three of my teens.)

So we got our teen a phone. Not a smart phone with Internet capabilities as originally requested – just the basic phone with texting capabilities. We explained to everyone that we'd decided it was more convenient for *us*. And, we didn't relax on the grade battle. When that teen was old enough to get a learner's permit to drive we held firm by requiring eligibility for a good student discount before driving could begin.

Another instance involved privacy. We raised our children to respect each other's privacy. That included not reading snail mail, email, and texts as well as respecting the sanctity of personal space such as bedrooms (knocking before entering, no snooping). But one of our teens crossed our unbreakable box boundaries and broke a law. It was serious and only by God's grace legal charges were not filed. *That teen* forever lost the privilege of privacy. I made it known that at any time I could and would invade previously private space and search as I felt necessary. In addition, I randomly asked for and read texts. Lastly, home Internet privileges were also suspended (we changed the home Wi-Fi password) for a period of months.

Another example regarded money. Our rule was if you earned money or received money as a gift, it was yours to do with as you pleased. But after one of our teens made dangerous purchases, we no longer allowed that teen to have money. I kept it "on account" in a small notebook in my purse, and when needed for whatever reason, I would dole it out. That meant all pay and monetary gifts were immediately given over to me for safekeeping. (Teens are much less independent when they have little cash in hand.)

See The Dangling Carrot for more about consequences.

> *Children are a gift from the LORD;*
> *they are a reward from him.*
>
> *Psalm 127:3*

TOOL: Mean What You Say

WRONG:

YOU: "You've lost Internet privileges *for the rest of your life!*"

Or:

YOU: "You're grounded until you're thirty!"

For me, consequences serve three purposes.

1. They should be an acceptable punishment for unacceptable behavior.

2. They are a deterrent for future unacceptable behavior.

3. <u>They are proof that you are fair, firm, and consistent regarding what you say and how you behave.</u> (SEE Dangling That Carrot.)

One of the greatest compliments my teens paid me went something like this:

> "I told my friend, you're lucky you don't have my mother. If she caught you doing that she never would have let you get away with it. When my mother says she'll do something, SHE MEANS IT!"

Here are my rules for consequences:

1. <u>Do the crime, pay the time</u>! Timeframes are hard and fast. Make sure that all consequences are structured under realistic timeframes. (A one month consequence that in reality will only last six days before you give in is far less effective than a one week consequence that goes from Friday to Friday no exceptions.)

2. <u>Consequences are no fun for anyone.</u> (Turning down free tickets to a once in a lifetime sports opportunity because of a grounding will probably break your heart almost as much as your teens'.)

3. <u>Consequences are appropriate, fair, and consistent</u>. Consequences should be appropriate to the age and ability of the child. First time offenses should carry a lighter consequence than third time

offenses. What if you're on your thirty-third offense? You're technique is broken. You need to reevaluate your rules.

4. <u>Consequences are most effective when they are discussed in advance</u>. The best ones are written down and signed by all parties involved (or posted in a prominent place) so there is no confusion over what exactly was agreed to. (SEE Let's Write That Down.) For example, I never expected all A's on a report card, but felt it fair to expect regularly completed homework. There was a consequence if that wasn't achieved.

5. <u>Keep it as simple as possible</u>. When our oldest teen got the first computer with Internet in a bedroom we discussed acceptable and unacceptable websites. My husband went through a lengthy discussion about the whys and wherefores and how our teen would be held responsible even when friends were over. It was a great speech but it was long and you could gradually see our teen's eyes starting to glaze over. I finally said, "I measured the monitor and it fits out the window. Any problems, that's where it will go ." Everyone knew I was serious, too.

6. <u>There is never any confusion for anyone over the consequence and the reason for it</u>. "I'm grounded but I don't know why or for how long." What good is that?

TOOL: The United Front

> "Let me talk to your father and we'll get back to you."

<u>Under no circumstances let your teens come between your partner and yourself.</u>

- Agree with your partner that you will not disagree in front of your teens (you can argue with each other and hash out things later in private if you have to).

- As much as possible, discuss situations *in advance* with your partner and come up with a game plan that you both feel comfortable with. (When it's not possible, use the phrase highlighted above.) My partner and I often roll play situations...

- Never, ever change a rule or a consequence that your partner has made. IF a change needs to be made (after you've had your heated, private discussion), (SEE Being Wrong) come back to your teens and say,

> "We've been thinking and we've decided instead ..."

TOOL: Let's Write That Down

> "I never said I'd do that."

Or:

> "You never said that."

Remember, you're always wrong and there is no way you can get them to see your reality. So debating what you did or didn't say guarantees an argument that will end in no one will win. For really important things, get your teens to write down the agreement and sign it. File it away or stick it on the kitchen bulletin board. I did this a lot for long term situations (I wouldn't let my teens get driver's permits until they were able to attain grades high enough to qualify them for a Good Student Discount on our car insurance, which saved us $400 a year. This took a full school year - a looooong time for teens.) If they refuse to write it down, you write it down, tack it to the bulletin board and say:

> "This is what I've heard us both agree to. Speak now or forever hold your peace."

<u>TOOL: The Dangling Carrot</u>

At one really low point in our home, one of our teens had no phone, no Internet privileges, and was grounded ... for months. Then that same teen got in trouble again ... and we had nothing left to take away. Talk about feeling helpless.

The key to effective consequences (I try not to call them punishments) is to know what matters to your teens and to make *wise use* of that knowledge. We didn't do that ... before therapy.

Good consequences are serious, nonnegotiable, and something that your teens would like to avoid. Like a carrot dangling in front of a reluctant donkey, a good consequence keeps your teens moving in the right direction. Good consequences have these important characteristics:

1. <u>Your teens have to believe that you will follow through on the consequence</u>. That means you have to believe it as well. Don't offer a consequence that everyone knows will never be administered.

2. <u>The consequence should offer incrementally worse options for continued infractions</u>. This gives your teens an opportunity for a "second chance" and, perhaps, a "third chance". (Perhaps your teens don't believe that you'll follow through ... and you do. Now your teens have some new information regarding you

and your "new" parenting style. They also know that the next time the consequence will be even more severe).

3. <u>The consequence must matter to the teens and, should it occur, cause the teens significant inconvenience and angst.</u> It probably will cause you significant inconvenience and angst, too, so be prepared. That phrase, "This hurts me more than it hurts you," could in fact be true. Think, "What is the single most important thing that matters to my teens?" and go from there.

4. <u>The consequence (and the rule it pertains to) should be discussed in advance and written down and visible for all involved.</u> Avoid confusion and further debate. Behave as if this is a contract between you and your teens. A "legal" agreement. No emotion need be involved. Just the facts, ma'am.

Consequences involve loss of privileges and loss of freedom. At times, consequences can be rather unique and creative to suit your teens and your family. At one point, right after a very bad time with one of our teens, I was actively looking at alternative schools for that teen to attend. This teen knew I was serious and desperately did not want to attend a different school. We were all glad that we never reached that point.

Remember:

1. You will only be successful when the consequence has a <u>significant impact</u>.

> "I don't care. I didn't want to go to that party anyway. Everyone there is a loser."

2. You're not going to be successful if you reach a point where there is <u>nothing left to take away </u>from your teens and they're still getting into trouble.

3. You're not going to be successful if your teens know that three days into a two week grounding <u>you're going to soften</u> and let them go to the concert anyway. (SEE Mean What You Say.)

4. <u>Stay United</u>! You're not going to be successful if your teens know that one adult in the house is less likely to follow through on rules and consequences than another adult in the house. (SEE United Front.)

How to Avoid Arguments

Talking with my teens often felt like I had fallen down the rabbit hole in Alice in Wonderland. I would be determined not to lose my temper or my train of thought, and before you knew it I was  completely off topic screaming like a banshee. I struggled with my teens' selective memory, distortion of the facts, and incredibly ignorant solutions to real problems. I had a strong desire to get my teens to stop looking at me like the enemy and to get them to understand where I was coming from and why. I failed almost every single time, and the level of hatred that bloomed in my family reached truly dangerous proportions.

UNFORTUNATE FACT: Teenagers live in a world of absolutes … or at least talk and behave like they do. "You *always…*" "You *never…*" "I'll *never…*". They absolutely believe the accuracy of their perceptions.

REALITY: Parents cannot alter this reality with words, actions or deeds.

TOOL: Jumping In The River

Instead of arguing – or going against the flow of the conversation – you jump in the river and go with the flow. These statements, made by your teens, though hurtful and technically incorrect, sometimes have a vague possibility of the truth. By acknowledging your culpability you literally take the heat out of your teens' fight.

> "You lie all the time."

WRONG:

YOU: "I do not! How dare you say that to me!"

TEEN: "You do. I know you're lying when I ask you how you are and you tell me 'fine'. I know you're not fine. It's not hard to tell when you're upset about something, you know."

RIGHT:

> "I'm sorry you think that's true. Can you give me some examples?"

TEEN: "I know you're lying when I ask you how you are and you tell me 'fine'. I know you're not fine. It's not hard to tell when you're upset about something, you know."

How To Avoid Arguments   [60]

YOU: "You're right; sometimes you ask me things that are private or that I don't want to talk about. From now on I promise to tell you exactly how I feel. But, be prepared. If you ask some questions that I don't want to answer I may say, "It's not your business," or "I don't want to talk about that right now," and you'll have to respect that."

When I use this technique my favorite part is watching the look of confusion on my teens' faces. They are so ready to get into a heated discussion over the ridiculous claim they've made and I just completely diffuse the attempt with my non-combative response. This is a perfect example why lying never helps your case. (SEE Honesty Is The Best Policy.) The hardest part about this technique is not becoming a bit smug and sarcastic a little ways down the road:

ALSO WRONG:

YOU: "Why are you asking me how you look? What do you care? Why would you want my opinion when you believe that I lie all the time?"

Have those snide comments in your head if you must, but keep from speaking them aloud. (SEE Do As I Do)

Here's another example:

> "You don't know what you're talking about! You have NO CLUE what it's like to be a teenager today."

RIGHT:

> "You're absolutely right. But I want to understand. Help me. What can I do?"

Here's another example:

> "You always say you're trying to do better the 'next time' but you never do!"

RIGHT:

> "I know I've made a lot of mistakes. I'm sorry if I've hurt you. But I'm trying to get it right now. What is one area you'd like us to work on?"

TOOL: The Volley

This tool is similar to Jumping In the River (in fact, both of these tools are interchangeable). This tool, however, passes whatever issue your teen has back to the teen in a precise, non-confrontational manner. I use this when the things that are being said by the teen are purposefully cruel.

> "You never let me do anything I want to do. All I am ever allowed to do is what

you want to do. I'm a prisoner in this family!"

WRONG:

YOU: "That's not true! How can you say that?! We bought you that new tennis racket and paid for lessons when you asked last spring. We just got you that brand new camera with all the fancy attachments when you decided you wanted to take up photography. We have this argument all the time ..."

RIGHT:

"I'm sorry you feel that way. What's your point?"

You've got to teach your teens that approaching you in a confrontational manner is not going to get them *anywhere;* you won't lose your temper, you won't argue, in fact, you won't even really converse. In refusing to join in to a no-win debate, you put your teens in a position where, if they really want something from you, they have to reevaluate their delivery. You retain power, you retain your calm, and you retain control of the situation without putting your blood pressure up.

Here's another example:

"You always favor Vance and Debbie! You are a lousy mother and always will be."

RIGHT:

> "I'm sorry you feel that way. What's your point?"

Here's another example:

> "I can't wait until I'm eighteen and can move out of this hell hole."

RIGHT:

> "I know you're unhappy here. All of us are struggling. What's your point?"

Adding "fuel to the fire" by arguing back (SEE When The Umpire Throws A Punch) benefits no one and will always make the situation worse. Keeping calm, diffusing the situation, and refusing to join in the fray is taking the "high road" and will work in your favor in the long run.

<u>TOOL: Not Always Being Right</u>

Acknowledge the fact that sometimes you are wrong. When you are wrong, don't hide it from your teens, acknowledge it and apologize for it.

You'd be amazed at how far that one small gesture will go sometimes.

> "I'm sorry I was so snippy and sarcastic last night. Please forgive me."

Or:

> "I'm sorry I was so short with you when you called. I was trying to solve a crisis at work. I'm calling you back now. Next time I'll say, "Can I call you back?" That would have been a lot better."

TOOL: My Reality vs. My Teen's

I had to come to the understanding that if my teens believed that the sky was green there was nothing that I could do to change that opinion. I stopped trying to. What did I care if my teens wanted to believe such an inaccuracy? The important thing was for me to maintain my Unbreakable Box boundaries so that I could stay sane.

In addition, I came to honestly believe that some promises teens make, even though *we know* they are impossible to keep, they actually – at that time – think they can do it. (SEE Living In The Moment.)

That means that as they are making that promise, they believe 100% that they can and will keep it. When you refute it, you're in essence calling them a liar to their faces. (Not a good way to have a positive discussion with anyone.)

> "I swear I'll keep my room clean from now on if you let me get a boa constrictor."

WRONG:

YOU: Oh, yeah? How many times have I heard *that* promise before! Want me to remind you? Remember when you promised to keep your room clean if I let you get that new carpet? I haven't seen that carpet *in the last year* there is so much junk on your floor. How about when you promised to keep your room clean if we let you get that new chair? Maybe you don't know you have a chair in your room since you can't see it. And while we're talking about you keeping your room clean, let's talk about some other promises you've made that you haven't kept ...

RIGHT:

> "I know you believe this and I honestly think you are absolutely sincere in making this promise. My reality is I've yet to see something like this really happen. How about you keep your room clean for the next two months and we'll talk again?"

How To Avoid Arguments

Don't be afraid to distinguish verbally between your reality and your teens'. Put it right out there that both of you are on two separate planes and that for now your reality takes precedence. Don't argue about who's reality is more accurate, either. That's an argument you are never going to win.

The disparity in your two realities does not have to become an unsolvable point of contention. Take the doubts you have regarding success which are based on hard facts and gently turn your doubts around. Think honestly, "What would it take for me to let my teens (fill in the blank here regarding what your teens want and what you seriously need from them)." Set up conditions with your teens to (hopefully) allow your teens to eventually succeed and gain what they want *on your terms and with your blessing.* (SEE Getting That Snake.)

Here's another example:

> "They're colored contacts. My friend brought them back from North Carolina for me. Everyone is wearing them. They're perfectly safe!"

RIGHT:

> "I'm sorry but my reality is that first and foremost I need to keep you safe. I called our eye doctor and they're very dangerous. They can cause infection and blindness. You

> cannot wear them. Give them to me. I'm throwing them out."

TEEN: But I paid $30 for them!

YOU: I'm sorry about that.

TOOL: Compromise & Cooperation

No one likes a dictator. Do you behave like one with your teens? Do you still have the same rules in place that you did when your teens were little? The teenage years are the perfect time to begin the art of compromise. Honestly communicate your fears and concerns and ask your teens to offer solutions. Giving them the opportunity to negotiate and come up with an acceptable plan is a vital life skill.

> "I'm sorry, Nancy. I just don't feel comfortable with you going to that party! I don't know the girl who is having the party nor do I know her parents."

TEEN: "How about I get you their phone number so you can talk with them?"

YOU: "Well, that would help, but anyone can sound okay on the phone. I'm sorry I'm such a worrier."

TEEN: "Would you pick Tania and me up after school tomorrow? Then you could at least meet her."

YOU: "Well..."

TEEN: "And how about after you talk with Tania's parents and meet Tania, then you can drop me off at the party and even come in for a minute if you want, plus you can call me anytime you need to over the course of the night, and then you can come and pick me up at midnight."

YOU: "What happens if I call and you don't answer?"

TEEN: "You can come get me. Immediately."

YOU: "11:00. Not 12:00. That's too late."

TEEN: "11:30? Please?"

YOU: "Okay. I will get to meet Tania and talk with her parents on the phone. I can drop you off at the party and come inside briefly. I can call you whenever I'd like and if you don't answer the phone I can come right over and get you. And you will be picked up by me at 11:30. Right? Thanks for helping me feel better with all this. You know I love you."

TEEN: (Eye roll and a put out sigh over how painful it is to have you as a mother.)

Compromising occasionally, if possible, on little things may go a long way for future successes. It takes you out of the role of always being the bad guy and sometimes you can work it to your favor in the future.

I've made a number of references to one of my teen's desire to get a pet boa constrictor throughout this book and how that wish has yet to be granted. In my opinion the arguments against getting boa constrictors (they live a loooong time and what about college?, you have to feed them live food and who will buy it?, etc.) are substantial. None of these concerns were a significant enough deterrent to my teen who had a solution to every one of them (the boa would go to college, securing a job would enable my teen to buy the food, etc.).

In my home there is a pet rat and a pet guinea pig though.

Despite our initial misgivings regarding the horrendous state of the bedrooms and the horrors of adding another living creature into that mess we decided to compromise and allow these pets. I got the same begging and pleading for these pets as well as the same promises.

My reality, that the promises would never be kept, was immediately proved true. My teens now have unimaginably messy bedrooms and pets. I suppose the object lesson is available at any time should I

How To Avoid Arguments   [70]

wish to prove my point that my teens don't always keep their promises.

But the rat's a clever, lovable thing and my teen adores her. The guinea pig is litter trained and comes when I call him. The cages are cleaned regularly without my interference, and picking up a bag of food is a lot better than the boa alternative. In the end it was a successful compromise for all involved and provided a nice "safe" area to converse and interact with my teens. (The rat rides on my shoulder in the mornings when I make school lunches and the guinea pig keeps me company running around the kitchen when I'm cooking.)

How To Improve Communication & Trust

It's the most important element necessary for a successful relationship and often it is the most problematic area between parents and teens.

UNFORTUNATE FACT: Teenagers don't like lectures, rarely want to engage in serious discussions with you, and in general feel that you cannot possibly understand them or their lives.

REALITY: You still have to talk to each other occasionally.

TOOL: Change The Way You Talk

WRONG:

YOU: "You need to start following through on your commitment to help me around the house."

<u>Pay attention to the way that you speak to your teen.</u> Remember, your goal is to communicate. Not order. Not make a point. Not prove someone right or wrong.

Conversations that begin with confrontational tones of "You need to...", "You must begin...", "You can't ...", "I will not allow ..." will immediately put your teens on the defensive. Your conversation's chance for success has been severely compromised before you even have begun.

Be open. Be honest. Share your authentic thoughts and feelings. Revealing your perspective, emotions, and needs to your teens will model similar behavior.

> "I was really looking forward to you helping me around the house like we talked about."

TEEN: Yeah well I didn't know that I was going to be a slave! I didn't realize I have to clean up all the dishes all the time!

YOU: That wasn't the deal. What's wrong?

TEEN: It's not fair! No one is cleaning up anything and when I come down the kitchen is completely destroyed!

YOU: Absolutely that's not fair. Let's talk.

Listen with an open heart. If you are fortunate enough to hear your teens say something revealing ("I'm afraid...", "I'm angry...", "I'm nervous ...") then make it your mission to try to allay these concerns. "What can I do?" "How can I help?"

"My lit teacher is making me insane."

WRONG:

YOU: "Oh, don't be silly.

OR:

YOU: "What are you talking about?! I've heard great things about Mrs. King!"

OR:

YOU: "You say that about all your teachers. What else is new?"

OR:

YOU: "Oh boy, I can see it already: another failing grade."

RIGHT:

"Why do you say that? What's happened?"

TEEN: She assigned a project that the whole class is going to fail.

YOU: Tell me about it.

TEEN: Well, she handed out like one thousand papers and we're supposed to....

Listen. Ask questions and gain facts. Learn. Talk.
Did you have any similar experiences growing up?
How did you solve them? Offer to provide
assistance.

<u>Make every conversation a fresh opportunity for
progress.</u>

WRONG:

YOU: I can't believe I have to have this
conversation again with you, Pam. It's like a never
ending loop.

OR:

YOU: Here we go again. (With an eye roll, too.)

> "Okay. I'm all ears and ready to listen.
> What's up?"

TEEN: I failed another math test and you have to
sign it.

YOU: Didn't you go for extra help?

TEEN: I <u>told you</u> it wouldn't work. I still failed.

YOU: Yes, but look at your grade! You improved
your score significantly! You <u>almost</u> passed! That's
an improvement, don't you think?

TEEN: It's still an F.

YOU: Let's take a look at the test and see what you improved on and what still needs more work...

Improving communication with your teens can only lead to an improved relationship with your teens.

> *Direct your children onto the right*
> *path, and when they are older, they*
> *will not leave it.*
>
> *Proverbs 22:6*

TOOL: Choose Your Battles

Hair grows back. Piercings do close up. Bright red bedroom walls can be painted over. Only take a stand about things within the realm of your Unbreakable Box. Everything else ... well ... ask yourself if it is really worth a battle. If you have a few core areas where you simply will not negotiate, you have a stronger case than if you are still seeking to control almost every aspect of your teen's life.

> "I don't think that's a wise decision. Do you want to hear why?"

The teen years are the time in which your teens are supposed to discover who they will be once they reach adulthood. You can try to guide them, offer them sincere advice, encourage them to take one route versus another route, but in the end sometimes *they just have to find out the hard way.* Sometimes, the opportunity to say, "This was what I was hoping to help you avoid..." carries more weight than, "I refuse to let you ruin your life by making such a ridiculous decision!"

> "I was worried this would happen when you decided to drop that math course. That's why I encouraged you to let us get you a tutor. Do you want me to help you find a summer course you could take to help make up the credits you still need?"

You must begin to allow your teens to make their own mistakes. Much of your wisdom is based on the mistakes you made and learned from. Your teens will learn the same way.

One last thing. You must <u>never</u> let them or help them escape the consequences for their actions! (We have even notified the school when one of our teens broke school rules and asked for their help and advice.)

> "I love you and I'm sorry you have to deal with this. I know you're frightened. We'll go with you to police station and be with you when you talk to the officer in charge. But you have to go. You left the scene of an accident and that's wrong and unacceptable."

TOOL: Repeat That

Sometimes in the heat of the moment we hear things incorrectly. Sometimes, we say something to our teens and they say, "Uh-huh," and we have absolutely no confidence that they comprehend and *will remember* what we've just said. Sometimes our teens say something to us and we just cannot believe what we have just heard. It never hurts to clarify. When trying to make sure everything is accurate and understood, get the other person in the discussion to do the repeating. Here are some examples:

> "Let me see if I get this straight. You're asking me if you can drive with three other girlfriends to upper New York state Friday to stay overnight with a family neither of us has ever met. Saturday, you want to go to an outdoor, all day concert and, even though you're not old enough for admission, and your friend knows someone who is going to sneak you in past the guards. Then, when the concert is over – probably close to midnight or one in the morning – you plan to drive back home and I should expect you home at about four a.m. Is this what you've just told me?"

Or:

"I know we've discussed the house rules regarding curfew and overnight arrangements; in fact we wrote them down. Before we start this discussion, just remind me what you remember about them."

Or:

"Why don't we start this discussion with what you know to be my primary concern in all the decisions I make regarding you?"

Or:

"What was our agreement regarding all this?"

TOOL: When You Get a Free Moment

So you've thought through something thoroughly: you've prayed about and discussed the subject with your partner. You know exactly what you want to say; your decision is final. You want to have a serious conversation with one of your teens about this issue but you expect that your teen will tune you out or blatantly disrespect you regarding what you have to say.

> "I need to speak with you about something that's been bothering me and that I've been praying about. Let me know if today at two or five is good."

(This allows your teens some say in how the conversation will play out. It's not "all you" making your demands/pronouncements on them.)

TEEN: "Okay. Let's talk."

YOU: "No, you've just gotten home from school. You're tired. You probably want to relax for a bit. It's okay." *Definitely decline the first time if your teens are willing to talk right away. You're in a better position if they must push you to begin the conversation.*

TEEN: "What?"

YOU: "Are you sure? It's really important to me and I really want to talk about this." *You've given them the freedom to choose the time and yet still categorically stated the importance of the discussion.*

TEEN: "Yeah, I'm sure. We can talk now."

Begin your discussion. I have found that by using this technique, your conversation begins on a better note because you've given your teens some power to dictate when the conversation happens. I've even tried texting something along this line (but refused to discuss it by text) and was delighted to have my teens initiate the conversation upon getting home.

TOOL: Listen and Learn

I had to learn to take whatever opportunity I could find when my teens spoke with me. Often it was during a time when I was stressed or busy and couldn't really afford the time. I *forced* myself to *make the time.* If I was at the computer, I stopped typing and either turned away from the screen or shut the computer down altogether. If I was watching television, I turned it off. If my teens were doing something and began conversing with me as I was passing by, I pulled up a chair and sat down and talked.

After a conversation like that, I tried always to follow up later, "How's Katie doing now?" or "Is Irene still grounded?" or "Is Michael still dating that same girl that he went to the prom with?"

TOOL: Make It A Date

My teens and I started to do small things together. (It actually started while driving to the therapist!) I'd buy a snack on the way and we developed favorite stopping places. There was no agenda and no hard questions asked; it was just time spent together. Then I made sure to talk (SEE Sideways

Conversations) about how much fun we had going
out for a treat now and then. It gave us a
foundation for discussion about things other than
the gigantic problems we were dealing with. It was
fun to laugh at crazy drivers, listen to music, and be
forced to talk about our day to each other.

TOOL: Believe It

> "You always take their side. You never
> stick up for me. You never believe me."

You probably have endless arguments with which
to defend yourself. Don't bother, because your
teens *will not* hear them or believe them.
Remember, they have an alternate reality and
there is nothing you can do to change it. You must
embrace the truth that your teens *honestly* believe
this statement.

WRONG:

YOU: "How dare you! That is completely untrue! I
treat all of you equally and fairly. I work very hard
to be as unbiased as I can. I can't help it that you
are the one that regularly gets caught in lies, that
regularly gets suspended from school, and you
have just been caught stealing money from my
purse!"

RIGHT:

> "I'm sorry you feel that way. What can we do to change this? Do you have any suggestions? I really want you to feel that I am listening to you and trying to understand your side."

Your teens will share additional information with you. Be prepared, they probably have examples that will hurt and you'll want to defend yourself – don't bother). Repeat the examples back so your teens know you heard them. (SEE Repeat That.) Then say,

> "Okay. Thanks for being open with me and talking. I didn't realize that's how you viewed those times. I'll make every effort to be careful to see <u>all sides</u> next time an issue comes up."

You've not admitted any guilt in that statement. Once again, your reality could be completely different. But you cannot dismiss what they have said if you want success. Look at this conversation as a very important glimpse into how your teens view you, your parenting style, and the situation they live in at home. Make an effort to be more sensitive in the future. Look for opportunities to consciously take your teens' side in the future.

TOOL: Praise

It really doesn't matter what it's about, but praising your teens each and every day is something you should seriously work to achieve. It can be as simple as making a fuss because they always remember to put their drinking glasses in the dishwasher or as big as acknowledging how skilled they are at conversing and interacting with an elderly relative. You've got lots to say about what they need to fix, what they need to stop doing, and what they need to remember ... add this one to your list as well.

> "You seemed so comfortable talking with Aunt Lois at Thanksgiving. You are so sweet to sit and listen to her stories over and over again. I was so proud of you, and you deserve to be proud of yourself."

Or:

> "Why can't everyone be more like Kate? She never forgets to put her dishes away in the dishwasher!"

TOOL: Take What You Can Get

Many teens never apologize. Never. Unless we insist on it (like we used to do pre-therapy) to which we'd get a sarcastic, insincere, "Sorry" which often only made the situation worse. But, that doesn't mean our teens aren't regretful for behavior or words that they've said or done. I've learned to take what I can get (it is better than nothing and often better than a simple "sorry"). Here are ways my teens apologize without ever saying sorry. If yours does this too, be thrilled with the effort and the sentiment and run with the opportunity when it's presented.

> "Want to go out for frozen yogurt after school?"

Or:

> "Want a cup of tea?"

Or:

> "There's a funny episode on TV. Want to watch it with me?"

Or:

> "Are you okay?"

On paper they seem small and innocuous but in reality they are wide, frustratingly brief openings that you should never let slip by unnoticed. Often, these opportunities are the most perfect time to make a fresh start on both sides.

TOOL: Asking Good Questions

Save your breath. When a situation arises that requires a discussion between you and your teens don't waste time voicing things your teens probably already know. Try starting your discussion with questions.

> "Why are we having this talk?"

Or:

> "What am I concerned about?"

Or:

> "Why am I upset?"

If you get a consistent "I don't know" to each of those questions, then ask:

> "Would you like me to explain things or shall we just discuss consequences?"

Giving teens some control regarding how the discussion plays out helps. You'll probably be very surprised with the answers you get.

Once the issue has been defined to your satisfaction, keep asking questions.

> "What did we agree on?"

Or:

> "What should you have done?"

Or:

> "What are the consequences we agreed on?"

Follow through on the consequences. Ask your teens if they need to say anything or have any questions and then move on.

Don't be self-righteous, indignant, or vindictive because they disobeyed. Deal with the behavior and move on. Staying calm, discussing the facts, expressing your love, concern, and determination to stick to your Unbreakable Box of standards is the key to keeping the conversation as effective as it can be.

It's the goal of all parents from the moment they bring their precious baby home from the hospital to try to get him or her to sleep through the night, right? Children develop the ability to speak, reason, and  disobey making parenting progressively more challenging. Like I said before, the teen years are your final exam. I found these few techniques wonderfully helpful.

UNFORTUNATE FACT: Rarely in life is anything 100% successful.

REALITY: You must never give up trying.

TOOL: Practice Makes Perfect

So, you're first big discussion with your teens after reading through this booklet ... is a complete disaster. Both you and your teens end up screaming at each other and things are said that shouldn't have been said. Don't ever expect perfection. Don't give up. Commit to trying again. Commit to facing reality and being honest.

> "Look, Marylynn, I really didn't want to end up in a screaming match with you last night. Honest I didn't. I'm sorry I lost my temper; I'm really trying to get better at that. Can we start over? ..."

Or:

> "Okay, Marylynn, last time we talked about this subject it didn't end well. I don't want to lose my temper and I don't want us both saying hurtful things to each other. I'm going to try some of my new tools to see if we can have this discussion without fighting..."

For God has not given us a spirit of fear and timidity, but of power, love, and self-discipline.

2 Timothy 1:6

TOOL: Post Hypnotic Suggestions

You probably think I'm kidding about this because I sure did the first time Marcia talked with me about doing this with my teens. It involves planting positive suggestions of behavior in your teens in the hopes of influencing positive future behavior.

Yes, it's manipulative; but it's positive manipulation and there's nothing wrong with that.

> "Sure you can go and sleep over Trinna's house on Friday night. Last time you went you kept me informed of what you were up to and remembered to let them know about all my crazy rules that keep me from worrying. Will you get me Trinna's mom's name and cell phone number again so I can contact her? I want to make sure the one I have is the right one. You were so good about doing that when you stayed at Kate's house the other weekend."

Your post hypnotic suggestion doesn't necessarily have to be perfectly accurate. (The "last time" I referred to could have been a heated discussion in which you succeeded in maintaining your "Unbreakable Rules" only through a lot of quick thinking and solid determination in the face of teen pressure. In the above example, I've given a complement to my teen implying that he or she *will* obey my rules and *will* keep me informed of what's going on over the course of the night. In addition, I've squeezed in that I *will* require the contact information.

Here's another:

> "Sure you can bake something. I know you'll clean everything up once you're done."

Even if this has *never before happened in your teen's lifetime,* there's always a first time. Especially if you've had discussions about the messes that were left behind in the past.

Or:

> "Sure you can go to the ballgame. I know you'll have your room picked up before you leave because you were so good about it last time.

Or:

> "Could you help me understanding something? You're so health conscious I know you'd never do this. Why would kids do such crazy things as taking random, unknown pills that someone gives them at school?"

Or:

> "Franchesca was telling me the other day how hard it is to work and get her homework done. I said, 'You should talk to David! He

> works all kinds of hours but always gets his schoolwork done no matter what!"

The key is to reinforce hopeful, positive future behavior. Then you can say:

> "Ha! Look at the grade you got on your pre-calculus exam! I can't wait to tell Franchesca how well you did!!"

TOOL: Sideways Conversations

I don't know about your teens, but my teens have ears like a bat. You can scream and scream that dinner is ready and they won't hear you, but whisper to a visitor, "That kid is driving me nuts" and you hear yelled from your teen's bedroom, "THAT PARENT IS DRIVING ME INSANE!" in response. I try never to have serious discussions about intense situations with others when my teens are in the house but that doesn't mean I don't have sideways conversations about them. Sideways conversations are post hypnotic conversations said to someone else about your teens with your teens in earshot. (More positive manipulation.)

> "Oh Debbie has such a tender heart towards the elderly and small children. It's truly a gift! I just love watching her interact and deal with situations that are difficult."

Or:

> "You should ask Sue. She's a whiz at computers – she can find anything."

Or:

> "Pam's been so patient with me and all my 'new therapy' techniques. I know she's laughing at me, but she's been sweet and willing to try. I know she wants things to be better between us just as I do."

It's a great opportunity to be positive about your teens and it goes a long way (trust me on this).

TOOL: Getting That Snake

For a period of time one of my teens wanted a boa constrictor. There was a constant litany about how my teen wanted a snake, but mom and dad wouldn't allow it, even though my teen had made endless promises about responsibilities, cost, care

... the list went on and on. Despite all of these sincere promises, still my teen's rotten, unfair, mean parents *wouldn't allow a snake!*

Now, I don't have any problem with snakes and my teen knew that was not the issue. My problem was that I *knew for a fact my teen would not have kept those promises.* So I flipped it on my teen. I came up with what *I wanted* to have happen in order for me to honestly and happily go with my teen to a pet store and get a snake.

> "Okay, Irene, you can get that snake. But here are the conditions I must have in order for you to get one. You have to keep your room clean – to my standards - for six straight months, no excuses."

TEEN: "Are you serious?"

YOU: "Yup."

TEEN: "That's it. All I have to do is keep my room clean for six straight months and we can go get a snake."

YOU: "Yup."

No, of course we don't have a snake. My teen never even made it a week. But my teen stopped asking for one and stopped putting the blame on us for not having one. I put the whole responsibility on my teen while at the same time keeping the power. No fights. No arguments. Just an honest agreement.

> "Okay Lesley, you want to participate in the senior class trip to Florida in two years? Let's talk about what I'm willing to do and what you're willing to do so that both of us can be happy about your going. Do you want to go first, or shall I?"

TOOL: Stepping Into The Fire

Both my husband and I struggled with Stepping Into The Fire and it took a long time for us to be confident about it. But it has worked *every single time.* This tool involves dealing with issues you'd rather ignore. Maybe these issues are very significant and you know that in addressing them there will be a tough discussion at best or a full blown knockdown, drag out screaming fight at worst. Maybe, it's something small and rather insignificant in the whole scheme of things, but significant to the overall well-being of the family. These issues between you and your teens, whether they are large or small, are the kind that are persistent and pervasive. They involve topics that you'd rather ignore and hope they'll go away ... or fix themselves. But, by ignoring them they just get bigger and more troublesome.

The pros for stepping into the fire are numerous. You can plan the discussion in advance and in a time frame of your choice. You can discuss how you will proceed with your partner and even role play where the discussion might go. You can reinforce your unbreakable box standards and you can have in place exactly how the rules will be enforced or modified.

Here's an example. The situation is that my teen was unreasonably angry with my husband for something he had done. Over a period of a week, this anger did not abate (as we'd hoped) but had festered and grown so that my teen is now angry, combative, and disrespectful whenever dealing with my husband. Who wants to make things worse by having another argument? Who wants to apologize for something they feel needs no apology? Who wants to rehash something that was a ridiculously small nonissue (at least in parent perspective)?

But the teen's anger and disrespectfulness is pervasive and showing no signs of abating. It's interfering with the mood of the house, causing anger and hurt feelings for the parent in the line of fire, and the behavior is being witnessed by the other teens in the house. We decided to step into the fire.

> "I'm sorry my behavior the other day upset you. I know you don't like other's to see

> photographs of you. But I'm proud of you and I like showing you off to people."

TEEN: "You NEVER listen. I've told you this before. I've asked you not to show my pictures to people. And you NEVER LISTEN! This time you did it AT MY WORK!!! You had to know that I was going to be furious. I'm sick and tired of it."

YOU: "I know. I didn't even think. I'm sorry. I'll try to remember."

TEEN: "Yeah, like THAT'S going to happen. You never change."

YOU: "Hey. Be respectful. I said I'm sorry. I'll do my best to remember the next time I'm in that situation. That's the best I can promise you. I'm proud for others to know that you're my child. Please be polite and give me credit for apologizing."

After that discussion, our teen blew out of the room and went upstairs apparently still angry. We looked at each other and shrugged. Oh well. At least we had done our part, modeled good behavior, and in doing so, left everything in our teen's "court". Not ten minutes later that same teen came down downstairs to us. We spent over thirty minutes sitting quietly as that teen talked and chatted with us like it was no big deal. But it was a big deal to us. This interactive behavior was something that rarely happened *when things were at their best*. We knew it for what it was: an olive branch; an acceptance of our apology although the words were never said. (SEE Take What You Can Get.)

Or:

> "David, we spoke about you being in bed by 10:30 on school nights. That meant computer, video games and phone turned off. We know for a fact that you were still gaming this morning at 2:00 a.m."

TEEN: "I TOLD you, I'm not tired! I can't fall asleep! I don't want to just lay in bed in the dark. And don't tell me to read. I hate books."

YOU: "We're not here to debate with you. We set these rules and you agreed to them, including the consequences. We've taken your game console for a month. Please tell us what else we agreed on."

TEEN: "I don't remember."

YOU: "Well, everything's posted here on the kitchen bulletin board. Let me read it to you. First offense: loss of game console for one month. Second offense: loss of game console and computer for a month. Third offense: loss of game console, computer, and cell phone for a month. If we have a fourth offense we'll have to talk again.

Now, what would you like for dinner: spaghetti or tacos?"

In your anger, you might be compelled to take everything away all at once. Which makes a serious point, but you should always leave your teen with something ... that he or she could lose if there is a further infraction. This is an incentive to stick with the rules.

TOOL: No More Yes/No Questions

If you feel that your teens are regularly dishonest with you (a high probability), the first thing you should do is stop asking yes/no questions and begin to ask pointed, direct questions. Let's face it, if you're not getting the answers you seek, why bother?

I was stunned at how often this works successfully. Let me show you an example. Let's say money is missing from the container where you collect singles and change for lunchs. You know your teen took the money because you found the pile of singles in a pants pocket while doing the wash. (Please note that this technique often works even if you don't have solid proof.)

WRONG:

YOU: "Did you take money from the lunch money container?"

TEEN: "No."

YOU: "But money is missing."

TEEN: "I didn't take it! Why do you always blame me?"

RIGHT:

"You took money from the lunch money container. Why?"

TEEN: "I needed money to buy lunch."

YOU: "Forty-seven dollars?!"

TEEN: "Oh …"

OR:

WRONG:

YOU: "Did you leave the milk carton out on the kitchen counter?"

TEEN: "No."

YOU: "Mary Lou, you're the only one in the house!"

TEEN: "Maybe you did it. You forgot and left your keys in the car the other day, remember?"

RIGHT:

"Please stop leaving the milk out on the counter. Next time you forget I'll take money out of your allowance to pay for a new one when the milk spoils."

TEEN: (Eye roll, but no denial.)

(Oh, and make sure you buy the milk from his or her allowance!)

.

These are areas where you need to be careful. Almost every one of them involves you (and your partner) and is critical to honest, lasting success. They are, undeniably, also the hardest to do.

UNFORTUNATE FACT: None of us Is perfect.

REALITY: Claiming imperfection is not a viable defense.

TOOL: Understanding Family Roles

FACT #1: Everyone has a role in a family.

Some roles include peacemaker, trouble maker, baby, hero, fixer, intermediary... You can probably look at your family and add more to the list. These roles start early and can stay in a family forever.

FACT #2: These roles can be good initially but bad in the long run.

My role in our family was intermediary. Whether I was part of the situation or not I was often an intermediary between the kids as well between my husband and the kids. In some ways it was good; I could anticipate problems and head them off at the pass, or I could step in when a situation was getting out of hand and diffuse a potential disaster.

But it was also bad. I was always on; always involved – even if the situation had nothing to do with me. In addition, I prevented members of my family from developing their own communication skills. As my children got older, they didn't even bother speaking to each other, they'd just come to me!

> "Kate always hogs the television after school. It's not fair."

OR

> "Lesley left a mess in the bathroom sink. I'm not cleaning it out."

OR

> "Dad wants me to go to Home Depot with him. I don't want to go."

OR

> "Tell the kids I'll be expecting them to help me clean up the mess from the storm in the back yard."

Cautions

As things got more difficult in our household, I felt tremendous pressure to always be present so I could "keep things calm." When things blew up I felt responsible for not being able to prevent confrontation which made me feel useless, ineffectual, and depressed.

Marcia helped me recognize all this, and I determined to stop being the "official family intermediary." I decided to mind my own business and everyone else was going to have to mediate their own issues. Which introduced me to Fact #3.

FACT #3: Families will often force a member into a role – even if the member doesn't want to be in that role.

It was hard for me to keep my mouth shut (no surprise to those who know me). Family members would try to get me to assume my old role either blatantly or subtly.

> "Ask Mom. She knows."

OR:

> "Mom, what do you have to say about this?" (From my husband.)

OR:

> "Mom, you have to help."

Cautions

It was very difficult. I'd sit and watch things ebb and flow during situations in which I normally would have mediated. I had to learn to keep my mouth shut. I played this game with myself that my family was actually a sitcom I was watching on television. I'd also try to pretend that Marcia was sitting next to me, whispering observations in my ear and making suggestions.

I watched things go wrong between the kids. I watched things go wrong between my husband and the kids. But I also watched things improve. Gradually, because I was committed, the family got the message that in matters that didn't involve me they were on their own. I was complimented as well because a number of times I was asked after the fact, "What would you have done?" or "Is there anyway you would have handled that differently?" Recognizing *my* family role, helped me become more conscious of the other roles in the family and attempt to adjust my behavior accordingly.

Seeing family roles more clearly and recognizing their significant influence on the dynamics in our home made a huge difference. The natural assumptions one would be inclined to make based on past history such as who was the root of the problem and who was the one that was blameless turned out to not to be as clear as I'd believed. I attempted to face each new situation with a "clean slate," giving my troubled teens the benefit of the doubt and trying to see things from their perspective while at the same time recognizing that none of us were perfect.

Cautions   [106]

When dealing with situations in your home, always remember to take into account the roles that exist in your family: how they impact members individually and the family as a whole. Is the "baby" being coddled? Is the "trouble maker" guilty before being proven innocent? Is the "perfect child" being given more credibility? Incorrect assumptions can hurt everyone. Fairness and impartiality are always the preferred attitude when dealing with emotional situations. (SEE When The Umpire Throws A Punch)

Ask yourself key questions such as,

- Are my decisions based on current facts or past emotions?

- Is this a situation displaying "typical" behavior for ... the "baby" or the "trouble-maker" etc.?

- Is this current difficulty the result primarily of family roles?

- Am I making assumptions based solely on past family roles?

- Have others in the family made assumptions based solely on family roles?

- Is this situation complicated by the fact that typical roles within the family have been disrupted?

Try imagining the identical situation with a different family member as the focus. How would things be different? How would things be the same?

Cautions   [107]

Watch out for expressions like this:

> "What trouble have you gotten into *this time*, Mike?"

OR:

> "Oh no. Not *again*. Some things never change with you, Vance. Why do I even bother?"

OR:

> "I'm sick and tired of having to deal with your mistakes!"

OR:

> "Suspended again? What else is new? I'm not surprised at all."

The opportunity for change – for both you and your teens – is readily available at every interaction between you and your teens. Don't miss your chance.

TOOL: Looking In The Mirror

Never expect any more from your teens than you are willing to deliver yourself. If you can't keep your temper during a discussion, don't be annoyed if your teens can't either. If you can't speak honestly about how you feel then don't expect your teens to. If you can't help being snide or sarcastic, don't expect your teens to avoid those behaviors. Do not, under any circumstances, qualify for the "Do as I say, not as I do award." You'll go down in flames.

Do not provoke your children to anger by the way you treat them.

Ephesians 6:4

TOOL: Fix What's Broken

One of the first therapists we met with after my teen came out of the hospital asked us in one of the first group sessions (me, my husband, and one of our teens) what we were hoping to get out of therapy. I said quite honestly and through my tears, "I want to figure out what we're doing wrong so we can fix this." She started to reassure my husband and I, and I interrupted her. "Look, we have three children. What we've done has worked moderately well for two of them but for this teen it hasn't. I know we are doing something incorrect but for the life of me I have no clue what it is. We need help. We need you to listen and learn and then tell us to stop doing this and start doing that. We'll do anything you suggest, *we just need to know what it is*." She looked at me and said, "Okay. Let's get started."

My husband and I committed to fix whatever was designated to need repair. We held back nothing. (SEE Not Always Being Right.) We answered loads of personal questions about ourselves and our teen. I'm sure our teen did the same thing from our teen's perspective. Were there any addiction problems? Was there a history of abuse? Had there been divorce? Separation? Infidelity? Was our marriage sound? Had our teen been adopted? Had our teen ever been removed from the home due to family issues? Did my partner or I have any physical, intellectual, mental or emotional problems? What was the family history regarding any of these topics? The questions went on and on and I answered as clearly and completely as I could. My husband and I met individually and as a couple with intake counselors, family counselors, psychiatrists, and nurses. We gave these people anything and everything they asked for and then waited for them to tell us what we needed to work on.

We were committed to fixing what was broken. As we were expecting our teen to do it, we could offer nothing less of ourselves.

Cautions   [110]

Hearing the truth of what our teen thought of each of us individually and as a couple was brutally painful. It still hurts to remember as I sit here writing this book. Imagine your worst enemy knowing intimate details about everything that goes on in your house and then telling it in detail to someone who then repeats it back to you in the form of fact finding questions. I was stunned to learn that I had been reported to the Division of Youth and Family Services for child abuse by my teen after slapping my teen. (DYFS had deemed my handling of the situation 'within acceptable limits' which was why I had never been contacted.) We learned in precise detail why our teen hated both of us. We learned specifically what our teen felt we regularly did wrong. And, hardest of all, we eventually learned from therapists what we had done that had made the situation worse rather than better.

The desire to get defensive is natural. Who wants to sit and have a stranger spell out what we should or shouldn't have done? The reality we regularly had to face was that we loved this teen of ours, and we refused to give up. We owned up to what we had to own up to and committed to fix what we were able to fix. We were determined that we would become better parents.

At our lowest times we clung to the fact that we had been moderately successful with our two other children. It was a stunning realization to us that what is successful with some children is not successful with all children. That's when I began to refer to my toolbox. I already had a good collection of tools that had worked well for me. But apparently I needed to find some new ones. In reality, I came to the realization that I needed a whole new system of tools. It was as if I suddenly had to convert to metric!

TOOL: Honesty Really Is the Best Policy

Don't lie. If you can't tell your teens something – or don't want to tell your teens something – then say,

> "I'm sorry but I can't discuss that with you"

Or:

> "Sorry, that's private."

Getting caught in a lie to your teens will affirm that your word can't be trusted and it's okay for them to do the same to you. (SEE Looking In The Mirror). If you already have a history of being untruthful with each other then sit down and have a serious discussion with your teens (SEE When You Get A Free Moment) and honestly tell them you want a fresh start. Remember: whether they are willing to join you is not as important as you sticking to your commitment.

TOOL: When The Umpire Throws A Punch

As hard as it is, it is imperative that during a discussion you make every effort to not lose your temper. When I talked with Marcia about how impossible this was, she gave me the illustration of a sports game with a referee. She pointed out that I *was not* an opposing team; I was the referee. The moment I lost my temper and joined the fight all was lost. This helped me change my perspective.

More help came when I continually reminded myself during discussions with my teens how almost everything they did was motivated by fear: fear of abandonment, fear of failure, fear of the unknown, fear of the future, fear of getting it wrong, and fear that they were going to end up unloved and alone. (SEE Understanding Fear.) I made myself recall what little I could about how difficult it had been for me to be a teenager and then honestly admitted how much *more* difficult it was to be one now. In addition, I worked to recall my teens as tiny little children who used to be afraid of big deer with antlers in their bedroom, blue tables, and blowing away in the wind. Those fears weren't rational but they were vividly real, and not something I could make go away no matter how hard I tried.

Cautions

Finally, the analogy of the referee reminded me of something: <u>I had the authority.</u> I wasn't an equal with my teens, I was the one that made the final decision. I knew what my boundaries were and that I should make any discussion with my teens very unemotional, cut and dried. (SEE The Unbreakable Box.) I was not going to try to change my teens' reality. (SEE My Reality vs. My Teens.) When unrealistic things were said, I wasn't going to get defensive (SEE Jumping In The River, nor was I going to argue (SEE The Volley).

The first time I had success with this technique was an amazing experience. I no longer felt embroiled but instead felt empowered. I participated in the discussion with my teens but I did not jump in. I was the referee, there to keep the rules in place and there to keep the game moving ahead in the direction it was supposed to go.

TOOL: No Secrets

At the beginning of this book, I spoke about refusing to live in denial. (SEE Embracing Reality.) Now, in addition, I wish to encourage you to be cautious when it comes to "family secrets" and "family privacy". I'm not telling you to take an ad out in the New York Times or start posting your family's trials and tribulations on Facebook. I am telling you not to be so concerned with appearances that you stay silent when you should speak up.

For instance, when I started seeing my therapist, I felt soooo much better. Immediately I began to feel that I was claiming power back, that I was more equipped, that the future seemed hopeful again. I'd tell people, "Well my therapist Marcia says..." or "You've got to hear how Marcia explained the reason why my teens..." I can't tell you how many people looked at me in shock and confusion. "I can't believe you're so open with everything that's going on with you," one person finally whispered to me in awe.

What exactly would I have gained to have kept all the bad stuff in? What benefit would I have achieved in failing to inform specific individuals in authority of what my teens were struggling with?

I needed to enlist people to my side and my teens' side to get them to pray for us, help us, give me information and advice, and work alongside us. In addition, I was delighted to discover that the more I spoke about things, the better I began to feel. I discovered that I was not alone with the family drama we were facing. And I actually helped some people by sharing what I learned. (Oh and nine so far: that's the number of people so far who have requested Marcia's name and contact information.)

When everything hit the fan in my house, I made sure I spoke personally with each of these adults informing them of all necessary information about my teens. This group included:

1. The <u>family physician</u>.

2. My <u>therapist</u> as well as my teens' therapist. (I also signed a permission waiver allowing them to speak with each other should they wish.)

3. My <u>minister</u>.

4. The <u>youth pastor</u> at my church.

5. A select <u>youth group leader</u> at my church who had regular contact with my teens, especially during overnight retreats.

6. My teens' <u>school counselor</u>.

7. I met with *all* my <u>teens' teachers</u> en masse for three consecutive years at the beginning of each school year and made sure they knew all the necessary history about our family.

8. <u>I signed a waiver</u> so that my family doctor, teen therapists, and school counselors could speak with each other about my teens. (HIPAA requires this.)

9. My <u>Bible study small group</u>. (For prayer support.)

Having no secrets from those who care about me and who want to help me and my family become healthy and strong and productive seemed like a no brainer to me. Knowing that everyone was on board and fully aware of my concerns gave me a wonderful level of peace.

TOOL: Avoiding Triangles

This one is interesting and addresses the nuances between family members. Have you ever been in a conversation with someone and the person you're talking with starts to talk in an unflattering way about someone else you both know? You're left in the rather awkward position of having to either go along with the trash talking (and then paint yourself in an unflattering light) or suddenly becoming a goody two shoes.

> "Daddy is so annoying. He just told me to clean up my mess by the couch. Do you see the pile of junk over by his chair? It's been there for over a week. He is such a hypocrite."

WRONG:

YOU: (*In the awkward position of just having had a heated "discussion" with your husband about the very real mess by his chair that has been there for over a week and with whom you are technically very annoyed at because you don't want to always be harping at two people to clean up.*) "I know, I love him but sometimes that father of yours makes me nuts. Have you seen his desk? And the back seat of his car? YUCK.

TEEN: "AND the basement! At least when you tell me to clean my stuff up we know that's because you're always the one that's stuck doing all the cleaning and keeping the house looking neat."

YOU: (*Feeling thrilled that you've not only received a back-handed compliment but your hard work at trying to keep the house clean has actually been acknowledged!*) "Oh don't even get me started on the basement..."

AND THIS IS WHY IT'S WRONG:

(*Later on that day.*) "Hey Dad, just wanted you to know that I cleaned up my mess. Better clean up yours. Mom says you're driving her insane with your mess all over the house, in the car, and in the basement. We were talking how you're way worse than I am."

This is an example of a triangulated conversation where two people "gang up on" a third person and it can only lead to problems. Here's what you should have done:

RIGHT:

"I hear what you're saying, Darci, but what are you going to do about <u>your</u> mess?"

TEEN: "Clean it up, I guess. But what about Dad's mess?"

YOU: "Dad's mess is Dad's mess. Darci's mess, is Darci's mess."

Here's another example:

> "Mom, I'm sick of Ron! It's bad enough he's a lousy brother and won't let me watch the movie I wanted, but I heard the way he was talking to you last night and that's just not fair. You were only trying to give him advice about college."

WRONG:

YOU: "I know. He's been positively awful to live with these last few weeks. He acts like he's the only one that counts in this house. I'm ready to scream. It's not fair how nasty he's been to everyone."

TEEN: "Do you know what he said the other day? He said he can't wait to get out of this house and away from you and dad and your constant nagging."

YOU: "Well, he better shape up and remember who's paying his college bills and giving him a roof over his head."

AND THIS IS WHY IT'S WRONG:

TEEN: "Hey Ron, Mom says she can't stand having you living here. She says you're driving her nuts and she's thinking of kicking you out. She might not even pay for your college."

Cautions

Triangulated relationships only get you in trouble
and will promote bad feelings all around.
Remember how teens have a different reality and
don't always hear things accurately. It's always
best to keep negative comments about other
members in the house to yourself – or at least save
them for your trusted partner or adult friend.

RIGHT:

"I hear what you're saying. Feel free to use
the television in my bedroom if you'd like."

TEEN: "Well, I wanted to lie on the couch..."

YOU: "Sorry, you know the rules. Wasn't Ron
there first?"

When in doubt, ask yourself this question: Would
you be comfortable having the third person being
discussed in this conversation hear what was being
said? If the answer is no, you're in a triangular
conversation. Get out ASAP.

The Best News

As I became more and more adept at using my tools, I watched my relationship with my teens improve. Oh, things aren't perfect but they are so much better! That sense of failure and insecurity as a  mother lessened so that I no longer feared the next confrontation; I knew I could handle it. Better yet, I knew that if I didn't get it quite right, I was still significantly better off than I had been before. My self-esteem and self-confidence improved. My depression was no longer an insurmountable black hole.

But I noticed something else, too. I felt like I was a better wife, friend, sister, and daughter. Stunningly, my tools and the benefits that came along with them influenced other areas of my life as well. Here I thought I just needed help with my teens and was stunned to discover I had inadvertently improved other areas as well! That's because *I changed for the better.* And what you do in one area in your life then affects other areas.

And my faith grew, too. The thankfuls that I'd had trouble coming up with in the beginning were now bright shining stars in the passing darkness. The Bible talks about God giving us strength in the midst of our weaknesses and trials to develop our endurance and strengthen our character. I realized this struggle had done exactly that. Thank you, Lord.

> *My grace is all you need. My power works best in weakness.*
>
> *2 Corinthians 12:9*

> *We can rejoice, too, when we run into problems and trials, for we know that they help us develop endurance. And endurance develops strength of character, and character strengthens our confident hope of salvation. And this hope will not lead to disappointment. For we know how dearly God loves us, because he has given us the Holy Spirit to fill our hearts with His love.*
>
> *Romans 5:3-5*

Our Family Then & Now

I've made every effort to be open and honest with you while at the same time respecting the privacy of our family. Yet I could not end this book without sharing with you a true, uncensored before and after glimpse of how far we have come. We're not done yet, we're still working on improving even more, but we are *so much better!* Just like our walk of faith, our family is on a continual journey with the determination to *get it right* as often as we can.

> *I don't mean to say that I have already achieved these things or that I have already reached perfection. But I press on to possess that perfection for which Christ Jesus first possessed me. No, dear brothers and sisters, I have not achieved it, but I focus on this one thing: Forgetting the past and looking forward to what lies ahead, I press on to reach the end of the race and receive the heavenly prize for which God, through Christ Jesus, is calling us.*
>
> *Philippians 3:12-14*

A Few Final Words

OUR FAMILY CIRCUMSTANCES PRIOR TO THERAPY:

- Homicidal thoughts towards those in authority
- Death threats to teachers
- Clinical depression
- Suicidal thoughts
- Opiate addiction
- Psychopathic and/or sociopathic tendencies
- Oppositional Defiant Disorder
- Conduct Disorder
- Complete breakdown of communication
- Fights – physical and verbal
- Theft of drugs, alcohol, money and possessions
- Psychiatric hospitalization
- Mistrust, deceit, and lies
- Confusion
- Concealed weapons: knives
- Obsessive Compulsive Disorder
- School suspension
- Pathological lying
- Bullying/emotional abuse
- Tears, fights, hatred

- Rage
- Despair
- Fear

OUR FAMILY CIRCUMSTANCES WITH THERAPY:

- High school graduation
- College enrollment
- Honor Roll, Awards
- Dean's List
- Family vacations
- Arguments with resolution
- Better understanding
- Medication for treatable problems (depression, OCD) with successful results
- Coping techniques and problem solving tools
- No more fear
- Gainful employment
- Improved relationships with friends, family and colleagues
- Conversations, laughter, listening
- Helping others with similar problems by sharing our family's story
- Stronger faith
- Healing

- Exciting, numerous future plans
- Healthy growth and change
- Repaired relationships
- Stunning moments of grace
- Healthier marriage
- Healthier friendships
- Healthier family relationships
- Healthier individuals
- Improved communication
- Improved self-confidence
- Optimism
- Tolerance
- Peace
- Wisdom
- Joy

Remember, you are never, ever alone. I memorized the following scripture passage during the darkest times so I always had it with me.

When I think of the wisdom and scope of God's plan, I fall to my knees and pray to the Father, the Creator of everything in heaven and on earth.

I pray that from His glorious, unlimited resources He will give me mighty inner strength through His Holy Spirit.

And I pray that Christ will be more and more at home in my heart as I trust in Him. May my roots go down deep into the soil of God's marvelous love.

And may I have the power to understand, as all God's people should, how wide, how long, how high, and how deep His love really is.

May I experience the love of Christ, though it is so great I will never fully understand it. Then I will be filled with the fullness of life and power that comes from God.

Now glory be to God! By His mighty power at work within me, He is able to accomplish infinitely more than I would ever dare to ask or hope.

Ephesians 3:14-20 NLT (with Lee Brooks tweaks – I made it first person.)

Resources

Contact and ask for information, guidance, and help from:

- Your local church
- Your local mental health center
- Your local city and/or county government office
- Your local hospital
- Your local doctor
- Your local school district

Each of these should have a wealth of information, specifically geared to your geographic location, that they should be able to direct you to.

WEBSITE: Psychology Today -
http://www.psychologytoday.com/ - This extensive website offers a wide variety of information regarding therapists, therapies, and issues. Organized by geographic location, the information provided enables you to find reputable professionals (for individual and group therapy) just where you need them.

WEBSITE: Mental Health of America -
http://www.mentalhealthamerica.net/ - the
leading advocacy organization addressing the full
spectrum of mental and substance abuse
conditions and their effects nationwide, works to
inform, advocate and enable access to quality
behavioral health services for all Americans.

WEBSITE: Parents Without Partners -
http://www.parentswithoutpartners.org/ - the
largest international, nonprofit membership
organization devoted to the welfare and interests
of single parents and their children. They may join
one of the many chapters around the US and
Canada; they may be male or female, custodial or
non-custodial, separated, divorced, widowed or
never married.

The Internet: Search online for blogs, specific
websites, reading material, and other useful
resources about your particular needs.

Schooling Qualifications

The information recorded in the following sections
was found on the Psychology Today website.

Clinical Social Worker/Therapist Clinical social
workers commonly hold a master's degree in social
work (or the equivalent) and have completed two
years of supervised practice to obtain a clinical
license. They may use a variety of therapeutic

techniques, including psychodynamic therapy or cognitive-behavioral therapy.

LSW The Licensed Social Worker has a graduate academic degree, has completed supervised clinical work experience, and has passed a national or state-certified licensing exam.

LCSW The Licensed Clinical Social Worker has a graduate academic degree, has had supervised clinical work experience, and has passed a national- or state-certified licensing exam.

MSW The Master of Social Work degree typically requires two to four years of study. This professional works with an individual in the context of the wider community, helping those dealing with domestic violence, child abuse, drug abuse, or foster-care issues, among many others.

Psychologist Psychologists in the US hold a doctoral/post graduate degree in psychology (in Canada some may only have a master's degree). Psychologists who practice typically will have completed their graduate training in clinical psychology, counseling, neuropsychology and educational/school psychology. Psychologists are required to complete several years of supervised practice before becoming licensed.

PhD The Doctor of Philosophy is an academic degree earned in four to seven years. Many psychologists, therapists, counselors, and coaches hold a doctorate of philosophy. A PhD in psychology emphasizes theory as well as statistics and data gathering. Psychologists with a PhD are also fully trained in the assessment and treatment of all behavioral conditions. (American Psychological Association)

PsyD The Doctor of Psychology, PsyD, is an applied clinical doctorate that emphasizes the application of psychology in a wide range of clinical settings to promote mental health. Training typically lasts between 4 to 7 years and includes 3 to 4 years of supervised clinical work experience. An individual who earns a Psy.D. in clinical psychology from an accredited program may become licensed to diagnose and treat mental disorders, conduct assessment and complete psychological evaluations, present expert testimony, and provide psychotherapy. This type of professional has a medical degree and can prescribe medications and usually works in tangent with other therapy professionals to determine the right medication needed.

MA A Master of Arts is a postgraduate academic degree typically based in fine art, humanities, social science, theology, or other liberal arts areas of study. It usually requires two years of study along with a thesis. Many counselors and social workers hold a master's degree, and many Ph.D. psychologists earn a master's "en route" to earning their doctorate degree.

LPC The Licensed Professional Counselor has advanced training, a graduate academic degree, clinical work experience, and has passed a state-certified licensing examination. Counselors treat all sorts of problems: from alcoholism and eating disorders to relationship issues and depression.

Counselor Licensed Counselors have a master's or a doctoral degree in counseling or a related area and complete two years of supervised practice. In most States, they are licensed as independent providers of mental health services, including the diagnosis and treatment of mental and emotional issues, and use a variety of therapeutic techniques.

BCD The Board Certified Diplomat certification is granted to practitioners who demonstrate a high level of competency and experience in their field and have five years and 7,500 hours of post-graduate clinical practice (including 3,000 hours under supervision). BCD professionals can be social workers, counselors, psychologists, or other mental-health professionals.

NCC The National Board for Certified Counselors (NBCC) issues the National Certified Counselor certification. The NBCC certifies counselors who have passed the National Counselor Examination for Licensure and Certification (NCE). This professional credential requires an advanced degree in counseling, clinical training, face-to-face counseling, among other course work. (National Board for Certified Counselors)

PMHCNS Psychiatric Mental Health Clinical Nurse Specialist

CADC Certification for Alcohol and Drug Counselors requires a minimum of a bachelor's degree or the equivalent, substantial training in alcohol and drug education, and 4,000 hours of supervised counseling experience.

LMFT The Licensed Marriage and Family Therapist has a graduate academic degree, clinical work experience, and has passed state-certified licensing exams. Along with a two- to three-year master's program with a practicum and internship, LMFTs are required to complete clinical training in individual or family therapy. Some states require completion of 3000 hours of service.

FAACP Fellow of the American Academy of Clinical Psychology. Psychologists who pass the American Board of Clinical Psychology's Board Certification examination in Clinical Psychology are eligible to receive the FAACP credential.

ABPP Established in 1947, the American Board of Professional Psychology (ABPP) grants Diplomat certification to licensed psychologists who demonstrate an advanced level of competency and experience in their service specialty. To obtain this certification, a psychologist must undergo a rigorous written and oral examination process by a team of examiners certified in that specialty.

(SOME) Different Types of Therapies

These are definitions I found on the Internet. Do your own research if you need more.

CBT Cognitive behavior therapy (CBT) is a type of psychotherapeutic treatment that helps patients understand the thoughts and feelings that influence behaviors. CBT is commonly used to treat a wide range of disorders, including phobias, addiction, depression and anxiety.

EMDR Eye Movement Desensitization and Reprocessing, or EMDR, is a powerful new psychotherapy technique which has been very successful in helping people who suffer from trauma, anxiety, panic, disturbing memories, post-traumatic stress and many other emotional problems. Until recently, these conditions were difficult and time-consuming to treat. EMDR is considered a breakthrough therapy because of its simplicity and the fact that it can bring quick and lasting relief for most types of emotional distress.

HYPNOTHERAPY is a form of psychotherapy utilized to create unconscious change in the patient in the form of new responses, thoughts, attitudes, behaviors and/or feelings. It is undertaken with a subject in hypnosis.

HUMANISTIC The humanist movement in general also focuses on the idea that people are innately good and tend toward goodness. In a humanistic therapy context, there is presumption that the true nature of the human is to want to improve, understand himself, and reach high levels of self-perception.

COGNITIVE Cognitive therapy makes the assumption that thoughts precede moods and that false self-beliefs lead to negative emotions. Cognitive therapy aims to help the patient recognize and reassess his patterns of negative thoughts and replace them with positive thoughts that more closely reflect reality.

PYSCHODYNAMIC Psychodynamic therapy, also known as insight-oriented therapy, focuses on unconscious processes as they are manifested in a person's present behavior. The goals of psychodynamic therapy are a client's self-awareness and understanding of the influence of the past on present behavior. In its brief form, a psychodynamic approach enables the client to examine unresolved conflicts and symptoms that arise from past dysfunctional relationships and manifest themselves in the need and desire to abuse substances.

Bibliography

Psychology Today Website:
www.psychologytoday.com

MSG: *The Message*, By Eugene H. Peterson,
Copyright 2002, Navpress

NLT: *New Living Translation*, By Tyndale Charitable
Trust, Copyright 2004, Tyndale House Publishers
(All quoted scripture is from the NLT unless
otherwise noted.)

NIV: Holy Bible, *New International Version 2011* by
Biblica, Inc.

www.biblegateway.com

About The Author

Lee Brooks is just a woman who's continually striving after God's own heart, trying to get things right. Life we live is filled with trials and tribulations and "normal" is an illusion that doesn't really exist.

Her hope is based on a life beyond this earthly existence and she strives daily to head purposefully in that direction. She knows that she is not alone in this and that with God by her side she will be able to handle anything this earthly existence can throw her way.

Being a writer and speaker, she tries to share both her successes as well as her failures so that others can benefit from her example.

True joy in this life is only through God's continued love, guidance, grace, and mercy.

*I am not worthy of all the unfailing
love and faithfulness You have shown
to me, Your servant.*

Genesis 32:10a

22079630R00079

Made in the USA
Charleston, SC
10 September 2013